EXTREME TEAMS

EXTREME TEAMS

WHY PIXAR, NETFLIX, AIRBNB, AND OTHER CUTTING-EDGE COMPANIES SUCCEED WHERE MOST FAIL

ROBERT BRUCE SHAW

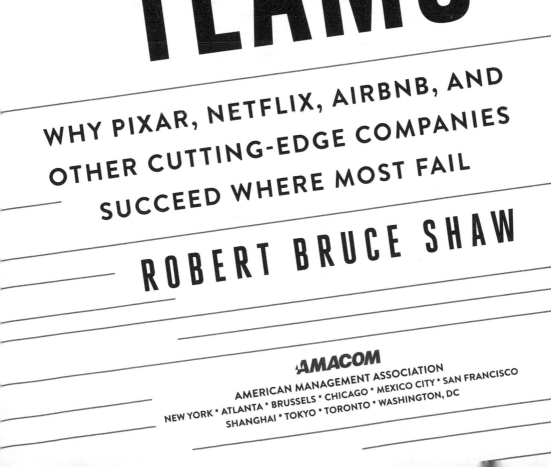

AMACOM

AMERICAN MANAGEMENT ASSOCIATION
NEW YORK • ATLANTA • BRUSSELS • CHICAGO • MEXICO CITY • SAN FRANCISCO
SHANGHAI • TOKYO • TORONTO • WASHINGTON, DC

Bulk discounts available. For details visit:
www.amacombooks.org/go/specialsales
Or contact special sales:
Phone: 800-250-5308
Email: specialsls@amanet.org
View all the AMACOM titles at: www.amacombooks.org

American Management Association: www.amanet.org
This publication is designed to provide accurate and authoritative information in regard to the subject matter covered. It is sold with the understanding that the publisher is not engaged in rendering legal, accounting, or other professional service. If legal advice or other expert assistance is required, the services of a competent professional person should be sought.

LIBRARY OF CONGRESS CATALOGING-IN-PUBLICATION DATA
Names: Shaw, Robert Bruce, author.
Title: Extreme teams : why Pixar, Netflix, AirBnB, and other cutting-edge
    companies succeed where most fail / by Robert Bruce Shaw.
Description: New York City : American Management Association, [2017] |
    Includes bibliographical references and index.
Identifiers: LCCN 2016043606 (print) | LCCN 2016053432 (ebook) | ISBN
    9780814437179 (hardcover) | ISBN 9780814437186 (eBook)
Subjects: LCSH: Teams in the workplace.
Classification: LCC HD66 .S4849 2017 (print) | LCC HD66 (ebook) | DDC
    658.4/022—dc23
LC record available at https://lccn.loc.gov/2016043606

ISBN: 978-0-8144-3717-9
EISBN: 978-08144-3718-6

10 9 8 7 6 5 4 3 2 1

To J. Richard Hackman
and his passionate quest to build better teams

CONTENTS

REVOLUTIONIZING THE WAY WE WORK

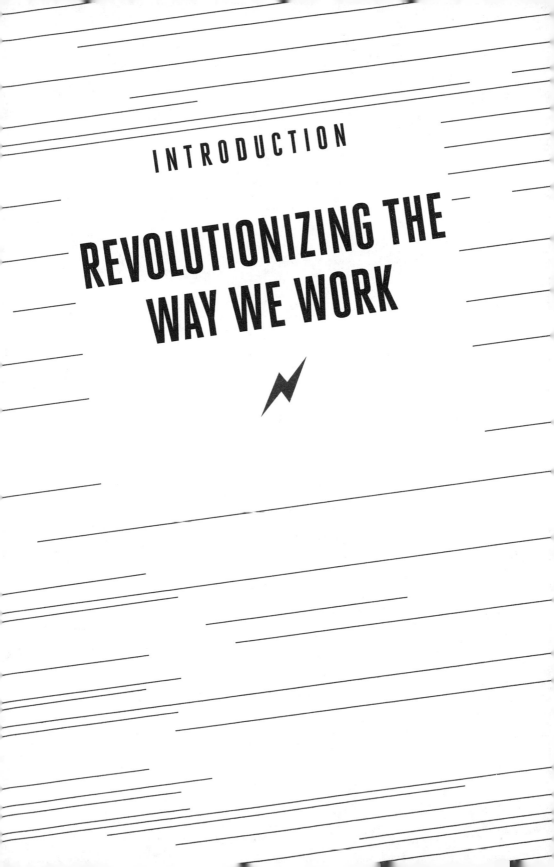

Imagine you are 22 years old, just out of college, and starting a new job. Further imagine being a foodie and your new job is with Whole Foods—a company second to none on its impact on what Americans eat. After all, how many multibillion-dollar grocery companies refuse to sell popular products, such as Coke, that they view as unhealthy? How many build a national supply chain for natural foods such as pesticide-free produce and organic milk? How many have standards for "clean foods" that are far tougher than those of our government? None—other than Whole Foods. The company is also notable in being viewed by employees as a great place to work.[1] Whole Foods strives to create a friendly environment where its team members share ownership of the success of the business and, in turn, share the benefits when the business does well.[2] The company offers a broad range of worker-friendly programs, such as profit sharing, team performance bonuses, employee health and well-being incentives, and time-off sabbaticals. One program, for example, enrolls team members in a weeklong clinic that includes health seminars, medically supervised health testing, discussions with nutritionists, and cooking classes. Whole Foods, in short, is a purpose-driven company that takes very good care of its people.

The company, now with 450 stores and 86,000 employees, is built around small, highly focused, and cohesive teams. Each new hire becomes a member of a team within a store—such as produce, meat, seafood, bakery, or prepared foods. These teams range in size from 10 to 50 people, depending on the work to be done and the size of the store. Each team operates in many respects as an independent business, making a range of decisions, including what products to offer and how they are promoted. Approximately 10 percent of a store's goods are ordered by headquarters staff in Austin, Texas, and another 30 percent come from the firm's 12 regional offices; all other product decisions are made by the in-store teams.[3] The degree of autonomy that these teams have in Whole Foods is exceptional in an industry where almost everything sold in a neighborhood grocery store is dictated by a few people sitting in a store's central headquarters office.

The teams at Whole Foods also have a great deal of power in the management of people. Consider that store employees are largely responsible for hiring new people. Job candidates are interviewed by a small group of team members. The interviewers ask focused questions regarding the job candidate's knowledge ("What are the advantages of locally grown produce?"), love of food ("Describe a meal you recently ate in as much detail as possible."), customer orientation ("Describe a time when you disappointed a customer. How did you fix it?"), and level of personal awareness ("If you don't get this job, why would that be the case?"). Gaining the approval of those on the interview panel is only the first hurdle that a job candidate must overcome. Each team, after working with a new hire for several months, votes as a group on who stays and who goes. In other words, the members of a produce team, not the team's leader or the store manager, will decide if a new member remains on that team. A new hire is voted out if team members conclude that he or she lacks what is needed to contribute to the team's success. The vetting of new members is treated seriously because teams are rewarded in Whole Foods based on team performance in areas such as overall sales and profit per labor hour. A team bonus is paid monthly, which can result in thousands of extra dollars each year for the members of a successful group.[4] Whole Foods then goes one step further. It posts each team's monthly results for everyone to see. A produce team, for example, will see how it stacks up on key performance metrics compared to the meat or seafood teams within its own store. Team leaders can also compare their team's performance against other teams across a region. New team members who do not pull their weight pose two risks. First, poor performers can reduce the bonus pay of all team members if the team's results suffer. That gets everyone's attention. Second, weak members can damage a team's reputation, as each team's results are posted within each store. Reputation is no small matter in a company where ownership of results resides with each team.

New hires at Whole Foods need two-thirds of their team members to vote "yes" if they are to remain with the company. In the vast majority of cases, new hires are accepted by their team. But there are cases where individuals fail to gain the necessary team support. For instance, one team member was rejected after he repeatedly took an overly casual approach to working with customers (such as putting his hands in his pockets and sitting on counters). He was warned by his colleagues to change his demeanor, but he failed to realize that this feedback from his peers was important. A Whole Foods manager described the dynamic within the company's teams: "There are people who are really good about working when the manager is on the floor . . . but as soon as the manager disappears, they lose control. . . . I'm not the one you need to impress. It's your fellow team members. And they will be as tough as they can be, because ultimately [the hiring decision] will be a reflection on them."[5]

Being "voted in" by one's new team fosters an emotional investment in the team's success and the overall success of Whole Foods. More generally, the company emphasizes the importance of team member happiness and a friendly work setting. Team meetings both in the stores and headquarters often end with what the company calls "appreciations." Team members, each in turn, express thanks for the support that another team member provided as they worked together or, more generally, his or her contribution to the company. While this can seem somewhat "new age" to those joining the company or to outsiders, the practice demonstrates the value the company places on positive team member relationships. One person commented about the culture of the company, "I never thought in a million years I'd work at a grocery store and feel so at home. Showing up to work every day, I'm happy to be here. When I leave, even if I'm exhausted from working hard, I'm still happy."[6]

Three guiding principles underlie the team environment at Whole Foods. First, the company believes that people are by nature social beings who feel most comfortable when part of a small group. From this perspective, building a company around teams is building a company based on human nature. Everyone in the company belongs to at least one team. The most basic are those working within each store. The leaders of these teams are members of the leadership group running a store. The leader of each store is also a member of a regional leadership team—and so it goes to the top of the company. But Whole Foods doesn't use teams simply to provide its employees with a sense of community. The firm believes that teams, when designed and staffed properly, also maximize what people can contribute to the success of a business. John Mackey, one of the firm's founders, set out to build a company that taps into each individual's creativity and potential:

> Working in teams creates familiarity and trust and comes naturally to people. Humans evolved over hundreds of thousands of years in small bands and tribes. It's deeply fulfilling for people to be part of a team, where their contributions are valued and the team encourages them to be creative and make contributions. A well-designed team structure taps into otherwise dormant sources of synergy, so that the whole becomes greater than the sum of the parts. The team culture of sharing and collaboration is not only fundamentally fulfilling to basic human nature, it is also critical for creating excellence within the workplace.[7]

Whole Foods, in sum, thinks teams when most companies think individuals. This is a profound difference that influences its policies, practices, and, most importantly, the way people think and behave within the company—including their interactions with customers. An executive of Whole Foods suggests that the firm's success is based on the experience of customers when they shop at its stores: "Customers experience the food and the space, but what they really experience is the work culture. The true hidden secret of the company is the work culture. That's what delivers the stores to the customers."[8]

A second management principle shapes how teams operate at Whole Foods. The company believes teams function best when they embrace a set of company-wide practices. Teams at Whole Foods have a great deal of autonomy to make decisions that benefit customers, team members, and the company. But they must follow a few standard procedures—for example, voting on retaining new hires or awarding bonuses based on company measures, such as team profit per labor hour. Whole Foods strives to keep its required practices to a minimum, believing that less is more when it comes to limiting what its teams can do at a store level. Whole Foods does, however, follow through on the practices it believes are essential—including a relentless focus on tracking and rewarding team performance. The company tracks a range of quality and service metrics.[9] Reviews are conducted once a month by outside staff to assess a store's performance in areas ranging from the presentation of its produce to the quality of its prepared foods. The results from these tours are reviewed with the store's leadership group, with the goal of improving how the store operates. Whole Foods augments these monthly tours with additional surprise inspections by more senior company executives.[10] Taking a full day, these reviews rate a store on more than 300 measures of quality, service, and morale—with the results posted each month for all stores to see. Whole Foods culture, then, has a surprisingly tough edge in forcing stores and teams to take full accountability for their performance. Whole Foods's calls this approach, one that gives teams freedom to operate within a set of shared company practices and metrics, its "democratic discipline."

A third guiding principle at Whole Foods is a belief in the benefits of being open and transparent as a company. The goal is to create a "no secrets" environment where information about its strategies and operations is available to all employees. The firm is designed to ensure that everyone is aware of how the company is performing and, in particular, how each team is performing. As noted, team results within a store are posted on a monthly basis. Also posted are in-depth financial reports for each store and for the company (which at the store level includes data such as sales, product costs, wages, and profits). The intent is to give people the information they need to operate at a high level—and foster a feeling of shared ownership among the company's members.[11] Whole Foods's belief in being as transparent as possible also extends to salary information. Team members can obtain the salaries of other employees, including the CEO. The firm believes that creating a high-trust culture requires sharing information that is concealed in most firms—and working with people to ensure that they understand the implications. For example, team members are encouraged to talk with their supervisors if they want to understand why someone else in the company makes more money or receives a promotion. The resulting feedback helps them understand how the company makes decisions and what they need to do to achieve their own career goals.

The company's team practices, and culture, evolved over several decades of trial and error—with leadership keeping what worked and abandoning what failed or had unintended consequences. The company, for example, refined over time how new hires were selected and trained. It experimented with how to best measure and reward team performance. It tried different approaches to providing the right balance of peer and supervisor feedback (including the use of 360-degree surveys). These practices were not part of a grand plan that its leaders executed when the company was founded. They knew that they wanted to build a new type of company, but its principles and practices were a work in progress. One lesson from Whole Foods is that experimentation with new approaches to teamwork is essential—that they are constantly evolving based on what a company and its teams learn based on experience. In fact, Whole Foods's CEO noted with a perverse pride that "We've been making it up as we've gone along."[12]

N

Most companies view teams and teamwork as a good thing. As a result, the use of teams is on the rise across all companies, with collaborative activities increasing by more than 50 percent over the past two decades.[13] Teams, without question, provide a competitive advantage when they operate well. The problem is that designing and managing teams is a complicated undertaking requiring a level of creativity and commitment that many firms, and their leaders, lack. The most basic, and common, mistake is to use a team when a team is not needed—that is, the work is better done by individuals not working as a team.[14] For instance, a group of leaders who are responsible for sales in different regions within a company can form a team. They develop a common set of goals and meet periodically to coordinate their efforts. The question to ask, however, is the value of this team in comparison to allowing the regional leaders to operate independently with little or no coordination other than reporting to the same supervisor. Since there is little overlap in how the regions in this company operate and no common work to be done, the value of a team is minimal if not negative (in consuming members' time that could be better spent elsewhere, such as interacting with customers). One way to express this is that the return on the investment of having a team needs to be greater than the benefit of not having a team at all. In some situations, the critical work to be done can be achieved more effectively by individuals or smaller subgroups. Consider the company whose strategy to promote growth is flawed. The leader needs to determine what role, if any, his or her leadership team will play in addressing this deficiency. Strategy development can involve an entire team or can be driven by a smaller, more specialized group from within the company or in partnership with an external consulting group. The decision of which approach to use is influenced by a variety of factors, including the skill of team members to think strategically and their ability to see beyond the firm's current business model. While it is logical to involve one's team, that may not be the best approach. A leader is sometimes better served by crafting the strategy outside of the team and then engaging the members in determining how to best execute it. My experience as a management consultant, perhaps surprising for someone writing a book about teams, is that teams are used far too often. In some cases, the best decision in regard to using teams is not to use one at all. Richard Hackman, a respected researcher of small groups, liked to remind those in love with teams that they inevitably create problems of coordination (determining how to work together to achieve a goal) and motivation (ensuring that everyone is engaged and contributing to the group's performance).[15]

A second mistake is failing to provide the support a team needs to be successful (such as group-level rewards). Even when the use of teams is warranted, many firms incorrectly believe that simply putting a group of bright people together will result in a positive outcome. How can a group of smart people not produce something worthwhile? Unfortunately, often too little thought is given to how a team is designed and managed. Even the most basic issues are ignored—such as careful consideration of who needs to be a member of a team and how it will define success. Companies often embrace teams, or at least the concept of teams, without providing attention to what is needed for them to be successful.

A failure to consider what a team needs to be successful extends beyond the team itself. To promote teams, organizations and their leaders need to carefully design the context in which they operate. Effective teamwork is often elusive because an organization's formal and informal systems contradict what a team needs. A common example is a reward system that works against teamwork. Microsoft, for example, required for years that its employees be ranked each year on a performance curve. On each team, only a particular number of people could be in each performance category, with the goal of identifying those who were underperforming and those who were stars. The result was that even in a team where everyone performed well, only the best of the best were rated in the highest category (which enhanced the pay and future opportunities of those individuals. As a result, some of the most talented people in the company did not want to become members of a team they knew would be staffed with other highly talented people—fearing that they could easily be rated lower when competing with such individuals. Those who did join the team knew that they were operating in what some call a zero-sum environment, competing with each other to receive the top ratings, which would be distributed across the curve. It is easy to see how such a performance rating procedure, designed to motivate higher levels of performance, would have the unintended consequence of undermining teamwork. This rating process, which was eventually discontinued within Microsoft, indicates that even actions implemented with the right intent can make teamwork more elusive within a company.

Let's assume that a leader uses a team when it is truly needed and works diligently to design it properly. Let's further assume that the organizational context in which the team operates also supports, or at least doesn't hinder, the ability of the group to perform at a high level. These are two essential positives. But it is equally important to realize that teams always come with a downside. Firms that use teams wisely are not naive—they know that teams, by their very nature, have negative qualities. For instance, research shows that some people will work less diligently when part of a team, allowing others in their group to compensate for their lack of effort. Social scientists call this the "freeloader" or "social loafing" problem.[16] In these situations, a few team members contribute less than others and yet benefit from being part of a team where others make up for their shortcomings. Whole Foods deals with this problem by having clear performance metrics and team-level rewards.

These practices, along with other informal methods such as peer feedback, increase the likelihood that everyone will contribute to the success of his or her team. New hires at Whole Foods quickly learn that they are not simply employees of the company or accountable only to their managers—they are, above all else, working for each other with financial and reputational consequences if they don't perform. Whole Foods, more than most firms, understands both what teams can contribute and where they can go wrong.

A final common misconception about teams, or at least high-performing teams, is that they are easygoing places to work. Some companies, including Whole Foods, contribute to this belief by emphasizing the benefits of a friendly work environment. Articles and books profiling these firms describe the fun side of how they operate—including a quirky work environment (colorful corporate offices, teambuilding events) and lavish benefits (free gourmet food, employee fitness centers, onsite massage). But what is often missing in the accounts of employee-friendly companies is the intensity of working in an environment where talented people, obsessed with their work, hold themselves and others accountable for producing results at a high level. Teams, when well designed, increase the pressure that their members feel to deliver for the group—to deliver for their peers. Realizing that your coworkers depend on you can be more stressful and messy than working in a conventional firm where people strive to gain their supervisors' approval.

$$\mathcal{N}$$

Consider Pixar. The well-regarded movie studio is known for producing blockbusters such as *Toy Story* and *Finding Nemo*. It is one of only a few studios that can attract an audience based on its reputation (that is, people will go see a Pixar film simply because it is a Pixar film). Those seeking to explain the extraordinary success of Pixar typically point to the role of its famous leaders—notably, Ed Catmull (cofounder and CEO), John Lasseter (cofounder and now chief creative officer, Walt Disney and Pixar Animation Studios), and Steve Jobs (who bought what became Pixar from Lucas Films and worked with Ed and John to build the Pixar we know today). These three individuals were clearly indispensable in Pixar's success. But it is a rare success story, Pixar or otherwise, that doesn't rest on the capabilities and performance of the teams within a company. Often unknown to people outside of a firm, they are the driving force behind a firm's success. This is particularly true because large and complex firms require more than any leader can provide—no matter how talented or charismatic he or she may be. This is not to minimize the impact of visionary leaders—it is, however, to suggest that the key factor in a leader's success, the area of his or her greatest leverage, is the ability to staff and support teams that a firm needs to grow.

Pixar's film *Toy Story 2* underscores this reality. The film, coproduced with Disney, was failing midproduction at an artistic level. The Pixar executives realized that a major overhaul of the film was needed, but it had to be done under a tight deadline. What followed was a nine-month race to create a film that met the release date but, more importantly, met Pixar's very high creative standards. Many of those working on the film were at the office seven days a week, month after month. During the intense period of completing the film, one of its animators drove to work one morning, thinking only of the work he needed to do that day. He forgot that he was to drop off his infant child at the daycare center. More importantly, he forgot that his child was in the backseat of his car. It was only when his wife called three hours later that he realized his mistake. He raced to the parking lot and found his child in the car seat—fortunately with no lasting harm. Pixar saw this event, along with an increasing number of repetitive stress injuries, as a result of employees spending hour after hour on their computers, as a wakeup call.[17] In particular, the firm's leadership saw the need to temper the willingness of highly committed people to do whatever it takes to produce a great film—one, in their words, that "touches the world."[18] The problem at Pixar wasn't that its people lacked motivation—the problem was that its people were too motivated.

What is sometimes overlooked in the *Toy Story 2* "parking lot" story is the benefit of having people who are obsessed with their work. This may be obvious, but it is worth repeating—having people who are consumed with a shared goal is almost always required to produce something great. Pixar's people care so much that they put themselves at risk of neglecting everything else in the pursuit of their shared goal. This can be a problem, as Pixar found out. Pixar's leaders tell the parking lot story as a cautionary tale of what can happen when you push people—or, more accurately, they push themselves—too far. They learned that they need to beware of aggressive timelines and the potential downside of having a highly committed workforce. The subtext of the story, however, is the pride of having people who are always at risk of pushing themselves and their teammates too far.

Pixar believes that producing great films requires something beyond having highly talented and committed people. The CEO of Pixar, Ed Catmull, notes that the key to success is finding people who can work well together.[19] This is particularly important on projects that can take three to four years to complete and literally require, over that time, thousands of decisions. Pixar believes, given the innovative and complex nature of its films, that success is unlikely if a team doesn't "gel." Or, stated in a more positive way, the making of a great film is dependent on a group of people bringing out the best in each team member and creating something beyond their individual capabilities. A common assumption is that people will naturally bond when they become members of a team. In fact, it is more likely that highly talented and driven people will have difficulty working together given the nature of their personalities. Passionate people are often demanding, stubborn, and idiosyncratic. Pixar, learning from experience, takes care to staff its teams with people who have complementary skills and personalities—people who can work in the intense and often ambiguous environment that comes with producing one of its films. Getting the chemistry right at Pixar is difficult—the company considers a range of factors, such as each person's background, values, and personality, as well as more mundane considerations, such as each team member's work habits. Pixar also wants a mix of people, some of whom have worked together and others who are new. The goal in striving to get people who can work well together is not to create a team of clones. In fact, having people who are too similar may make it easier for them to work together, but it will most likely undermine the team's creativity. The goal is to find a group of people who can bring their unique talents and experiences to a project and then come together as a team to produce something beyond what they could do as individuals.

All of this makes sense, but what happens when a team fails to gel? After all, team chemistry is not an exact science. Pixar operates with the assumption that the key to making a great film is getting the story right. Everything else is secondary. The firm further believes that the way to get the story right is to get the team right. Great teams produce great stories—not the inverse. Pixar has a host of practices to maximize the likelihood of a team pulling together to produce a great story. For example, the firm gives its teams very direct and sometimes tough feedback during the making of a film. This feedback comes, in part, from what it calls its "brain trust," a group of mostly senior leaders who have directed Pixar films themselves. This group, however, has no formal authority to mandate changes in a film. The goal is to provide feedback but not in a manner that takes accountability away from a director and his or her team for the quality of their film.

Pixar believes that a well-functioning team, even one that is struggling and "wandering around in the wildness," needs to be trusted and protected during the creative give and take of making a film. The job of senior leadership is to closely observe how a team is operating, with the belief that the quality of the team members' interactions is key in producing a great film. A team that is working well together is given more time and protection, even if it appears to have lost its way. A team that is fragmented and failing as a group needs to be changed. What are the signs that a team is failing? An individual who worked on a number of Pixar films noted that trust in the film's director is essential:

> Once trust starts to erode, it creates problems on a film. The signs of low trust are numerous: people stop showing up for meetings, or spend more time on their phones in the meetings. They will also be more likely to ask the leader to show them what they want—to have the director explain once again his or her vision. You also see people being rude to others, particularly in other functional groups. They are frustrated that the film is drifting and they take it out on those around them. A loss of trust also results in people not wanting to work on a particular shot because they believe the story will not pan out and their shot will be cut. They may work on the project but don't put their heart into it. The lack of commitment is clear in a creative culture like Pixar where emotional investment in a story is all important.[20]

Over the past 10 years, a significant number of Pixar directors were removed midstream from their films. This includes the directors of *Cars 2, Ratatouille, Monsters U, Brave,* and, most recently, *The Good Dinosaur.* The senior leadership of Pixar removed them from their jobs, in large part, because the directors had lost the confidence of their teams.[21] Pixar, of course, is not alone in being a studio that will replace directors midproduction. But it is important to note that Pixar views itself as being a different type of company—one that is "filmmaker led." The company prides itself on being more supportive and trusting of its people than other movie studios. Moreover, the firm's willingness to remove people is all the more remarkable given the close interpersonal relationships that exist within the company. Many of Pixar's key hires, particularly in its early years, were friends of those already working there. Friends hired friends who shared a passion for films. One story told to me by a person who worked at Pixar involved John Lasseter, one of the top leaders in the company. A film the studio was making was having difficulty getting its storyline right. It simply wasn't coming together. The film's director decided to drive from San Francisco, where Pixar is located, to Los Angeles for a set of meetings with Disney staff. Lasseter volunteered to ride with the director—allowing the two of them to spend time in the car working on the film's story. Lasseter, with no shortage of demands on his time, was willing to make the drive to fully support one of his people. This level of commitment was typical of the degree to which people in the firm cared about the films they were making and were willing to invest in the success of each other. John Lasseter noted that his company's culture was one based on deep relationships:

> The people at Pixar are my best friends. . . . Not only do I want to see them every day—I can't wait to see them every day—but, when my wife, Nancy, and I make a list of whom we are going to take on vacation, the top group is Pixar. We just want to be together all the time.[22]

Some firms don't encourage close working relationships among their members and, instead, operate in a less personal or emotional manner. Such firms can more easily fire people with less angst than a company like Pixar. It's not personal—it's business. On the other extreme, there are firms that encourage close working relationships among their members but will not take action, or timely action, when people fail to deliver what is needed by their teams or companies. Business, in these cases, takes a back seat to personal loyalties. The bonds among people get in the way of making the tough decisions often needed to move the business or project forward. Pixar, then, is unique in being softer than most companies ("The people at Pixar are my best friends") and also harder ("We will fire best friends when needed to make a great film"). One member of the company noted the dilemma this creates:

> Pixar can struggle at times with being honest about how it operates. The company is very supportive and has an emotional

culture. But it always puts story above people. If a director can't develop a story that meets the firm's very high standards, he or she is removed. They are typically offered other projects within the firm, or their old jobs back, but most don't stay. It is too tough emotionally to go back when you were just removed from your role because of a loss of confidence in your ability. This happens primarily to directors but it can cascade into other, less elevated, positions as well.[23]

A company like Pixar is both softer and harder than more conventional companies. One way that academics look at the "hard/soft" dynamic is to distinguish between communal and exchange relationships.[24] Communal relationships are those based on supporting others without expecting anything in return. In these relationships, people are bound together by emotional ties and mutual loyalty. Families operate based on communal relationships, where favors and support are provided to others without an expectation of immediate reciprocity. Exchange relationships, in contrast, are based on what others provide you and, in turn, what you provide them. They are based on a formal give and take—I provide you with something and you provide me with something in return. Most view businesses as being based on exchange relationships. Employees, for example, provide their ideas and effort, and, in return, a firm provides them with compensation, benefits, and career opportunities. These two types of relationships, communal and exchange, are viewed by most as mutually exclusive—that is, you exist in either a communal or exchange relationship but not both. This is the case because each operates with a different set of rules and expectations. From this viewpoint, a business that appears to be based, at least in part, on communal relationships is still, in reality, an exchange relationship (only with a softer edge).

The rigid distinction between exchange and communal relationships is a relatively modern concept. In the past, the two were closely intermingled in a wide variety of preindustrial businesses and families. For example, in Elizabethan England there were families that consisted not only of the husband, wife, and children but also those who joined the family as contracted apprentices and servants. This was particularly true for the households of master craftsmen (blacksmiths) and yeoman farmers (those who sold their crops in the marketplace). All of these people were thought of as members of the family and closely connected in the production of the family goods or agricultural products. An historian of the period describes these households as spheres of mutual interdependence, with the contributions of all required for the family, defined broadly, to be successful.[25] Still today, family businesses are found in great numbers in every part of the world, some of them growing to become massive companies. These firms range from small "mom and pop" shops to multibillion-dollar enterprises. They combine exchange and communal relationships in unique ways that address the specific challenges they face.

To say that cutting-edge firms and teams operate based primarily on the dynamics of exchange relationships is to miss the depth of communal bonds within these firms and, in particular, the importance that they place on relationships. These firms are hybrids—possessing both communal and exchange qualities. They blur in their own unique ways the distinction between exchange and communal relationships in a manner that combines the positive qualities of each. Patagonia, for example, was among the first companies in the United States to build an onsite daycare facility for its employees. The firm's goal was to support employees with young children and enhance the family spirit within the company. The founders believe that bringing together employees and their children in an onsite childcare center results in a stronger company culture.[26] Sometimes the blending of exchange and communal relationships is done because a firm's leader believes that it is the right thing to do—that a business must be more than a series of exchange relationships. But most of these firms also do so for more pragmatic reasons. Patagonia sees the business benefit of having a childcare center that helps attract and retain talented employees who want their children to be in a quality facility located where they work. That said, Patagonia did not spend the money to build and run the childcare center for its financial benefit—it did so because it was the right thing to do for its employee community.

Balancing exchange and communal relationships, however, is complicated. In particular, firms that treat employees as family run the risk that people will feel betrayed when the company treats them not as family but as employees. Research indicates that the greater the expectations of being treated as if they were in communal relationships, the greater the disappointment and even anger when that is not the case.[27] This means that firms that emphasize the importance of community and connectedness will be judged more harshly when they place other considerations above those relationships. For example, Pixar employees could believe their firm is being hypocritical in creating a warm corporate environment, a family where people care about each other, only to fire people when necessary. It would be much easier to simply create an environment that is formal and professional—one where there is no confusion regarding exchange and communal relationships. That, however, is not the way of cutting-edge firms. Pixar doesn't support close personal bonds for the sake of community—it does so because making great films requires emotional connections among those making the films. They need both exchange and communal relationships—and are willing to suffer the consequences of striving for both simultaneously. They deliberately take the harder path.

⚡

Whole Foods and Pixar are different firms operating in different industries, each with its own history, culture, and challenges. But they are similar in how they view and use teams. Consider the following:

➡ Both firms value teams and teamwork more than conventional firms, seeing teams as essential to their success. They view their companies as a collection of teams (versus a collection of individuals). These firms value teams because teams, as they use them, provide an advantage that competitors can't easily replicate.

➡ Both are deliberate in how they staff their teams, looking for people who are highly talented but also a good fit with their unique cultures. They want people who are passionate, even obsessed, about their work and also care deeply about their coworkers and their firms.

➡ Both understand the importance of team chemistry and work hard to create a sense of community within their teams. Each has formal and informal practices that strengthen the interpersonal bonds within and across teams.

➡ Both see the need for disciplined approaches to building effective teams, including the use of clear performance targets and rigorous work practices. People view Whole Foods and Pixar as "soft" cultures, but each has robust processes and practices where needed.

➡ Both make changes in their teams if they fail to produce results. Teams are provided with ongoing feedback and are expected to address performance gaps. Leaders, in particular, are responsible for staffing and developing teams that perform at a high level. They are fired if they fail to do so.

Cutting-edge firms, such as those profiled in the following pages, are those that understand the potential power of teams and are willing to experiment with new approaches. I call the teams operating within these firms *extreme teams* because they embrace bold new approaches that go beyond what is found in conventional firms. The seven companies profiled in this book are Whole Foods, Pixar, Zappos, Airbnb, Patagonia, Netflix, and Alibaba. I selected these firms based on several criteria. I sought firms with a track record of significant growth and financial success. Each of these firms has demonstrated an ability to grow and prosper, even in the face of adversity. Each outmaneuvered much larger competitors to assume a leadership role in its respective industry. Whole Food is the leader in the natural foods movement in this country. Pixar created an entirely new category of computer-generated movies and overtook Disney as the premier animation company in the world.[28] Patagonia has become one of the most respected providers of high-quality outdoor clothing, taking customers from traditional outfitters such as L.L.Bean. Zappos did what people thought was impossible by selling shoes on the Internet and, in the process, fighting off larger and more well-funded competitors.[29] Airbnb created a whole new category of hospitality and now offers more rooms each night than any of America's largest hotel chains. Netflix drove Blockbuster into bankruptcy and is now taking on media giants such as HBO in producing and streaming TV shows and movies. Alibaba outmaneuvered eBay in the emerging Chinese e-commerce market and is now one of the world's largest companies based on market value.

Another factor was important in selecting the seven firms in this book. I looked for firms that were willing to experiment with new approaches to teams and teamwork. These firms are constantly striving to improve how they operate with little regard for common operating practices. Whole Foods is willing to share the salaries of all employees among team members. Most firms take the opposite approach and keep salary information secret. Whole Foods believes in transparency and challenges traditional thinking in sharing salary information. These seven companies are constantly experimenting with better ways of operating—and don't simply replicate what others had done. In this regard, they are interesting firms with a level of energy and creativity often missing in more traditional groups.

Cutting-Edge Firms with Extreme Teams[30]

Pixar: Film studio operating as a largely independent division of Disney. Ed Catmull is cofounder and president. Motto: "Develop computer-animated feature films with memorable characters and heartwarming stories that appeal to audiences of all ages."[31]

- **Year founded:** 1986
- **Revenue:** Box office, $1.2 billion (2015 estimate)[32]
- **Number of employees:** 1,200

Netflix: Media company that provides customers with movies and TV series via streaming on the Internet. Reed Hastings is cofounder and CEO. Motto: "End boredom and loneliness," "Make people happy," "Win more of our members 'moments of truth.'"[33]

- **Year founded:** 1997
- **Revenue:** $6.77 billion (2015)
- **Number of employees:** 2,450

Airbnb: Online peer-to-peer marketplace for people to rent rooms, apartments and homes around the world. Founded by Brian Chesky, Joe Gebbia and Nathan Blecharczyk. Motto: "Belong Anywhere."

- **Year Founded:** 2008
- **Revenue:** $900 million (2015)
- **Number of employees:** 2,400

Whole Foods: Natural Foods grocer operating primarily in the United States. John Mackey is cofounder and co-CEO. Motto: "Whole Foods, Whole People, Whole Planet."

- **Year founded:** 1980
- **Revenue:** $15 billion (2015)
- **Number of employees:** 86,000

Zappos: Internet clothing company that is a division of Amazon. Focuses on shoes but also offers a range of attire. Tony Hsieh is cofounder and CEO. Motto: "Delivering Happiness."

- **Year founded:** 1999
- **Revenue:** $1.2 billion in 2009 (now part of Amazon—its revenue is not reported separately)
- **Number of employees:** 1,400

Patagonia: Outdoor clothing company with a strong environmental focus. Yvon Chouinard is founder, and Rose Marcario is CEO. Motto:

"Build the best product, cause no unnecessary harm, use business to inspire and implement solutions to the environmental crisis."[34]

- **Year founded:** 1973
- **Revenue:** $750 million (estimated 2015)
- **Number of employees:** 2,000

Alibaba: E-commerce company that serves business and retail customers. Jack Ma is founder and executive chairman, and Daniel Zhang is CEO. Motto: "Global trade starts here" and "Make it easy to do business anywhere."[35]

- **Year founded:** 1999
- **Revenue:** $15.69 billion (2015–16 fiscal year)
- **Number of employees:** 34,000

Leo Tolstoy observed that "All happy families are alike; each unhappy family is unhappy in its own way."[36] Teams appear to fit the Tolstoy mold in that the best teams have similar attributes while dysfunctional teams are unique in their ineffectiveness.[37] Many authors have examined the dynamics of dysfunctional teams, and there is certainly merit in understanding how these teams lose their way. The premise is that we can learn how teams can function better by studying those that fail—that by avoiding the "wrongs" of highly ineffective teams, we can build productive teams.[38] This assumption, however, is only half right. Avoiding the wrongs of troubled teams is necessary but insufficient. A truly high-performing team does much more than avoid common team mistakes—just as an extraordinary person does more than avoid the problems that fill the pages of an abnormal psychology textbook. I take a different approach in avoiding the discussion of team dysfunctions and instead concentrate on highly innovative teams. I am interested in the commonalities across these teams that make them successful, with a focus on the following practices:

1) **Fostering a Shared Obsession:** In extreme teams, members share a passionate belief in their work and the firm of which

they are part. They often have a cult-like quality, seeing themselves as unique and destined to improve the world. These teams also have a deep faith in their ability to overcome adversity. Contrast this approach to conventional teams whose members often view their work as tasks to be done, even professionally, but with no shared passion for their work or the team's larger reason for being.

2) **Valuing Fit over Experience:** Extreme teams value the personal traits needed for a group to achieve its goals. Each team develops a unique set of practices to ensure that members have the right mix of personal motives, values, and temperament. They hire and promote people who fit their culture. Those who have these traits are asked to join the team; those who don't are asked to leave. Contrast this approach with conventional teams where members are often selected based on their past experience or functional skills.

3) **Focusing More, then Less:** Extreme teams fixate relentlessly on the vital few areas that are critical to their success. They dedicate the vast majority of their time to these priorities and go to great lengths to avoid distractions (including unnecessary processes and controls). These teams, however, also develop approaches that provide the time, resources, and autonomy needed to creatively explore new opportunities for growth beyond their firm's current products and services. Contrast this approach to conventional teams whose members often focus on a wide range of priorities and are easily distracted by less critical demands.

4) **Pushing Harder, Pushing Softer:** Extreme teams are simultaneously harder and softer than conventional teams. The culture of these teams is tougher in driving for measureable results on a few highly visible targets. These teams are also willing to openly deal with their own weaknesses and take

action on those who are underperforming. At the same time, these teams are softer in terms of being more supportive in creating environments that foster collaboration, trust, and loyalty. Contrast this approach to conventional teams that are more "beige" in how they operate—failing to push either the hard or soft sides of effective team life.

5) **Taking Comfort in Discomfort:** Extreme teams are biased in favor of conflict, even encouraging it among their members. These teams believe that fighting over the right issues, regardless of the discomfort it causes, results in better outcomes. Equally important is the ability of these teams to take on big challenges and the risks associated with innovation. Contrast this approach to what is often found in conventional teams where people view conflict as something to be avoided or a sign of failure.[39]

Conventional Versus Extreme Teams

Conventional Teams . . .	Extreme Teams . . .
View work as a job to be done professionally	View work as a calling—even an obsession
Value team members' individual experiences and capabilities	Value members' cultural fit and ability to collectively produce results
Pursue many priorities at once—more is more	Pursue a limited set of vital priorities—less is more
Strive to create a culture that is efficient and predictable	Strive to create a culture that is at once both hard and soft
Value harmony among team members—striving to avoid conflict and discomfort	Value conflict among team members—recognizing the benefit of being uncomfortable

Let me offer a few caveats before moving on, in the following chapters, to the core practices of extreme teams:

➡ First, one can select different firms and teams as case studies using the same criteria I noted earlier (that is, selecting groups that are both successful and innovative in how they use teams). A host of well-known companies, such as Amazon, Apple, and Google, or smaller firms, such as Uber and Vice, are worthy of further examination in regard to their team practices. The firms included in this book are meant to be illustrative of new approaches to teamwork in a variety of settings, with the assumption that the team practices found in these firms are evident in other successful firms.

➡ Second, there are clearly differences among the firms profiled in this book, even though I describe them, collectively, as extreme teams. My intent is not to treat these firms and teams as replicas of each other but, instead, to look at their commonalities and then explore their differences in order to better understand the trade-offs each has made in successfully designing and deploying teams. For example, Netflix goes to great lengths to remind its people that they are part of a team and not part of a family. Families don't fire their children (as much as some, at times, might like to do so). Netflix views professional sports teams as the best metaphor for what it wants to achieve—a group where individuals are replaced by others if they can't provide what the group needs given the challenges it faces. In contrast, Zappos goes to great lengths to create a family-like ethos. It embraces a family metaphor in describing its culture. The Zappos website notes:

> We are more than just a team though—we are a family. We watch out for each other, care for each other, and go above and beyond for each other because we believe in each other and we trust each other. We work together, but we also play together. Our bonds go far beyond the typical "co-worker" relationships found at most other companies.[40]

Zappos wants its people to relate to each other at a deeper level than what is found in most conventional companies.[41] Zappos even requires its managers to spend significant time with team members outside of work—at events, dinners, and bars—and will not hire those who find this part of the Zappos culture unnecessary or uncomfortable.

➡ Third, the success of the companies in this book is due to a range of factors, not simply how they use teams. Teams are critically important to them, but other factors are as well. A flawed corporate strategy, for example, will doom a company even if its teams are operating in a highly effective manner. Whole Foods, for example, is one of the most innovative firms in the world in how it uses teams. But it is facing increased competition from larger organic stores such as Sprouts, as well as mainstream grocers such as Kroger and Walmart (who are now offering health-conscious customers lower-cost organic food). Amazon is also starting to sell food via its Amazon Fresh delivery service. Its mainstream competitors now threaten to undermine the Whole Foods business model and its ability to grow (at least at a rate comparable to the past). These threats will require effective strategic choices on the part of the firm's senior leadership. Whole Foods is now opening lower-cost stores under the brand name 365. The impact of these new stores on the success of the firm is based on the premise that traditional Whole Foods and its new sibling can coexist, without cannibalizing the sales of each other. Teams at Whole Foods provide a competitive advantage, but they are not more important than this type of shift in the company's offering, which will help determine its fate.

➡ Fourth, some of these firms, while demonstrating innovative team practices, may not stand the test of time. The history of business is one of firms that are successful for a period of time and then succumb to competitive challenges or their own self-inflicted wounds. Zappos has recently introduced a bold self-management approach called holacracy that has the potential to take the firm to the next level of performance—or undermine the success it has had to date. None of the seven firms profiled here are without flaws, and each has made significant mistakes over time. Alibaba failed to act as quickly as needed to deal with counterfeiters using its sites to sell their goods. Airbnb failed to respond effectively to safety issues when they arose in the early years of the company. Netflix failed to meet its customer expectations when it separated its DVD and streaming businesses. There is no reason to believe that these firms, as great as they are, will not make more mistakes as they move forward.

A variety of external forces can also undermine a firm's success. New technologies, for example, can overtake a firm. Netflix may see its business model eroded if augmented reality overtakes movies and TV as a dominant form of entertainment. At this point, we don't know how that technology will evolve but it may be as disruptive as Netflix was to traditional media companies.[42]

➡ Finally, a risk in profiling a set of exemplary firms and teams is that others attempt to mimic them. That is, some will identify a highly visible team technique from an exemplary firm and then implement it in a very different setting without understanding what is needed to make it work. In these cases, those incorporating new approaches are seeking positive outcomes without fully understanding how to achieve them. The specific team techniques described in this book must be viewed in relation to a particular firm, its history and culture, as well as its aspirations. For example, Whole Foods is one of the most team-based companies in the world. Other firms, given Whole Foods's success, might strive to broaden the use of teams in their own organizations. Teams should be used only when they add real value and can be supported effectively by their organizations. In some situations, teams shouldn't be used. In these cases, a company is better served by structuring work around individual responsibilities or using more ad-hoc teams than what is found in Whole Foods. Or firms might decide to implement "after action" reviews based on the success of this technique at Pixar. These reviews look at what worked and what didn't in a recently completed film project—with the goal of improving how the firm and its teams operate. However, the culture of the firm needs to be such that people will be honest in conducting these discussions—otherwise, the real issues are not surfaced and the reviews are largely a waste of time (or worse if the real problems are known but not surfaced). In looking at the teams in this book, a reader needs to understand the intent behind a particular cutting-edge practice and the broader environment that is needed to make it work—and then determine if and how to best use that technique in one's own company or team.

The difficulty of designing and supporting extreme teams is the reason they are a competitive advantage. If managing these teams was easy, they would be less valuable because they could be copied easily. There needs to be a great deal of thought, and perhaps more importantly ongoing experimentation, to get the formula right. The caveats mentioned here do not minimize what we can learn from cutting-edge firms. These groups are a work in progress, each trying different team approaches to determine what works for them. In that regard, they are worthy of our attention both for their willingness to experiment and their successes in doing so. That they have cast aside conventional wisdom may be the most important lesson for those seeking to improve their own groups. In creating teams that win, fortune does favor the bold.

TAKEAWAYS

> ➤ Cutting-edge companies are using teams in innovative ways to outperform their competitors. These extreme teams share five success practices. They . . .
>
> > ► Foster a shared obsession among the group's members
> >
> > ► Value cultural fit over experience in selecting new hires
> >
> > ► Focus on their vital few priorities while remaining open to new ideas
> >
> > ► Create a team culture that is simultaneously hard and soft
> >
> > ► Take comfort in the discomfort that comes with risk and conflict

CHAPTER

1

RESULTS AND RELATIONSHIPS

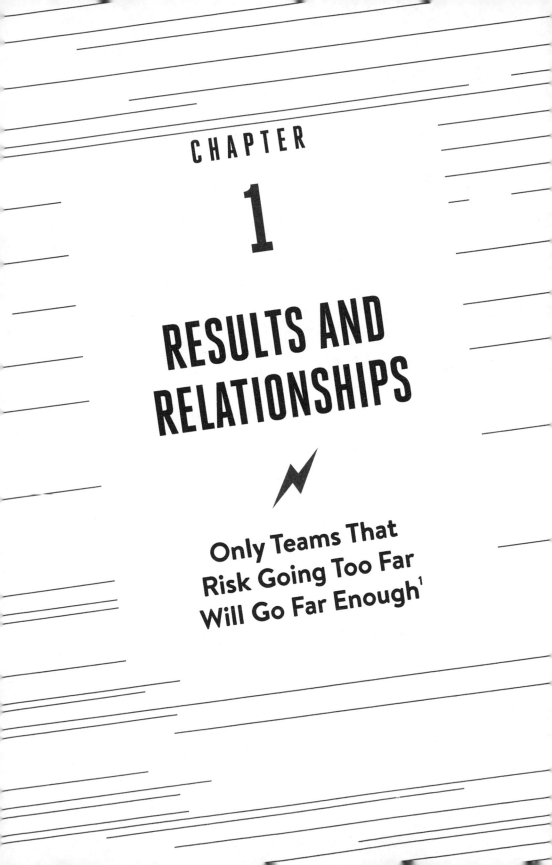

Only Teams That Risk Going Too Far Will Go Far Enough[1]

Netflix was born of a simple idea—provide movies on DVDs delivered via the U.S. Postal Service.[2] This was a radical departure from the approach of the industry leader at the time, Blockbuster, which had more than 9,000 stores filled with rack after rack of videocassettes. The founders of Netflix claimed that they started the company out of frustration with being charged $40 by Blockbuster for a movie rental turned in six weeks late. That story, however, was nothing more than a clever marketing ploy.[3] The truth was that the founders, already successful entrepreneurs, wanted to be the "Amazon of something."[4] They saw that DVD players, then rare, would come down in price and become the preferred technology for viewing movies. Netflix even worked with DVD manufacturers and retailers to accelerate that process. Once it occurred, people embraced the Netflix model—one that offered a vast selection of movies online, rapid turnaround of orders, and a simple low-cost fee structure. The bright-red Netflix mailing envelopes were soon appearing in mailboxes across the country. Blockbuster, which in 2000 was 500 times as large as Netflix,[5] was slow to respond to the Netflix threat—unable to believe that its greatest asset, a vast chain of retail stores, had become a liability. The decade-long battle between the two firms culminated in Blockbuster's bankruptcy—a casebook example of a nimble startup company outmaneuvering a much larger and well-established firm.[6] Netflix continued to grow and is the world's leader in the online streaming of movies and TV shows, with more than 83 million subscribers.[7] It is now moving aggressively into the production of original content with hit TV shows such as *House of Cards* and *Orange Is the New Black*. Netflix, with a track record of taking big risks in the pursuit of growth, will likely become the dominant media company in the world.

Netflix is equally bold in its approach to people management. More than 8 million people have downloaded a presentation of the firm's operating principles.[8] Sheryl Sandberg, CFO of Facebook and author of *Lean In*, suggests that the Netflix "culture deck" may be the most important document ever produced in Silicon Valley.[9] In it, the company describes how it operates and, in particular, its freedom and responsibility culture. Netflix believes in giving its employees a great deal of autonomy but also holding them to high standards of performance. Each year, it strives to do something that reinforces the freedom people have in how they work. For example, Netflix did away with the need for its employees to track their vacation time—they take as much as they need. The key ingredient in making this model work is having the right people. Freedom and responsibility are not worth a great deal if people lack the motivation and capabilities needed to deliver results. Netflix developed its culture deck after the firm's CEO, Reed Hastings, was dismayed after conducting new-hire orientation sessions where up to one out of three new people were shocked by what he told them about the firm's high-performance culture (emphasizing, in part, that they operated as a team and not a family and people need to continually earn their place in the company—otherwise, they would be fired). Hastings held some of his hiring managers accountable for not clearly communicating his firm's culture to those they hired. But he decided that putting the Netflix culture principles in writing would reduce the number of people who wondered, after joining the firm, if they made the right decision. He didn't want anyone thinking the company had engaged in a "bait and switch." The culture was not for everyone, and Hastings wanted new hires to be told what to expect.[10] The culture deck, as a result, was distributed to all potential hires and, thus, by default, became a public statement. Hastings decided to post it for those interested in how his firm operates.

Netflix uses the term "talent density" to describe the level of skill within a firm. High density is a workforce comprised of people who can perform at a level that Netflix describes as extraordinary. It developed the idea of density after the painful experience of laying off one-third of its workforce early in its history due to insufficient cash flow. The firm retained its most talented people and let go of the others. After the layoffs, the firm's leadership was fearful that the company would not make progress on its improvement initiatives because the remaining 80 employees would need to focus on simply running the existing business. But, to their surprise, the work to be done was getting done faster and better with far fewer people. Hastings, the CEO, commented, "We tried to figure out why. And we realized now there was no more dummy proofing necessary . . . everybody was going fast and everything was right."[11] A second insight from that period was that those who remained after the layoffs enjoyed working in an environment where everyone could be trusted to do an exceptional job. They wanted to work in a company that consisted only of highly talented people. The joy they felt from this experience was even more than the success that typically resulted from their collective efforts. The company decided then that it would develop an approach to ensure that it retained only extraordinary people moving forward—and not settle for mediocrity in any way.

Netflix believes that most firms suffer from the opposite—which becomes more pronounced as they grow. This occurs because mediocre talent can be tolerated when a firm is successful and has the financial buffer to carry those who are underperforming. In essence, large companies can afford those who are far from extraordinary (versus smaller startup firms that generally don't have that luxury). Netflix further believes that firms, as they grow, create processes in an effort to compensate for a decrease in talent density. Most large firms, for instance, require annual operating plans and conduct regular operating reviews to ensure that their various groups are focused on the right priorities (versus trusting them to do so more spontaneously). Each functional group (such as finance and human resources) develops its own set of processes with the best intentions, but the cumulative effect can create stifling bureaucracy. The problem is that processes are almost always less effective than talent in surfacing and adapting to emerging business challenges and competitive threats. Processes are based on a set of assumptions about what is needed in a given situation and a particular point in time—which becomes a problem when the assumptions on which those processes are based become outdated as things change in a firm's marketplace. This is not to suggest that processes are unnecessary—only that processes are no substitute for talent.

Netflix works hard to avoid the trap of putting processes before people. It gives its employees big jobs and ample latitude on how to perform those jobs. It strives to simplify or eliminate the administrative requirements it places on its people. It also works hard to surround its people with talented peers, which the firm believes is the best perk a company can offer employees. All of which is good news if you work at Netflix. The bad news, at least for some, is that Netflix will not only fire underperformers—it will fire those who are only average. Netflix believes that talent ultimately determines who wins in a competitive battle. The company is tenacious in upgrading talent because it believes the output of an extraordinary employee is 10 times that of an average employee. It also believes that the best thing it can offer its employees is the experience of working with other highly talented, highly dedicated peers.

The primacy of talent within its culture impacts almost all of Netflix's actions when it comes to people management. The company, for instance, recently introduced a generous one-year unlimited sabbatical for employees who are new parents. The program pays the salaries of those who want to spend time at home with their newborns. Their jobs are waiting for them when they return. In announcing the program, Netflix described the program as a means to attract and retain superior talent. It noted that:

Netflix's continued success hinges on us competing for and keeping the most talented individuals in their field. Experience shows people perform better at work when they're not worrying about home. This new policy, combined with our unlimited time off, allows employees to be supported during the changes in their lives and return to work more focused and dedicated.[12]

Netflix is now clear about its expectations—extraordinary performance from every employee. Effort doesn't matter. Intent doesn't matter. Results matter. This can mean, at one extreme, that those who produce outstanding results with relatively little effort are rewarded based on the outcome they achieve. On the other extreme, those who work hard but fail to produce results will leave the firm. This doesn't mean that they are fired after one misstep, but it most likely means they are fired if there is a second misstep. This firm's approach is all the more striking in that Netflix is competing for talent in a tight labor market. Silicon Valley has a low unemployment rate, with the competition for top-flight engineers being particularly intense. With talent in short supply, we might assume that Netflix would be more accommodating of average performers. Not so. The firm's emphasis on superior results begins in its orientation sessions with new hires. One employee, responding to a question about the firm's culture, observed:

> I currently work for Netflix—and yes, there is a culture of fear BUT it is pretty much outlined to you on DAY ONE that if you do not perform, they will find you and get rid of you as quickly as possible. So you know what you're in for as soon as you step in the door.[13]

Another employee, echoing the same sentiment but with a touch of dark humor, described a mythological "sniper in the building" whose job it is to locate and kill any Netflix employee who fails to deliver extraordinary results.[14]

Understanding the Netflix approach to talent is summarized in a story that Reed Hastings tells often. Early in his career, Hastings worked for a startup technology firm as an engineer. He would work long hours and neglect some of the more basic office tasks, such as washing out his coffee cups each day. Instead, he let them pile up, and then, at the end of the week, someone took the cups, cleaned them, and returned them to his office. Reed assumed the janitor was washing the cups and putting them back in his office. This went on for over a year until he came in one morning at 5 a.m. and found his firm's CEO in the bathroom washing Reed's coffee cups. Hastings was surprised and asked if he was the person washing his cups each week. The CEO said yes and that he did it because Reed was working so hard, including all-night sessions, and the CEO felt this was something he could do to help him. In telling the story, Reed said this small act of kindness made him want to follow the CEO to the ends of the Earth. And here is the story's punchline—that is exactly where he led the company. The CEO, great with people, was terrible at building products that customers would buy. Hastings's lesson—people skills are important, but the key is having the judgment needed for a company to be successful. The question that Hastings asks of himself and his managers, particularly in regard to talent, is, what does the company need to promote its growth and what decision is needed to move it forward?

⚡

A second defining trait of the Netflix culture is an ability to look beyond its current business model to the future. The company was planning on being the industry leader in streaming movies online while it was still working hard to win the DVD war with Blockbuster. DVDs were just a stop along the path to streaming. It was planning to produce its own TV shows and movies while it was still a distributor of content being produced by well-established studios. It was planning to expand internationally while it was still working to build a U.S. presence. This firm's focus on the future is only in terms of its business model—it impacts how it manages its people. Managers are told that their most important job is to build teams that deliver results. Toward this end, Netflix managers are told to periodically question the skills they need on their teams moving forward. The company, in particular, goes to great lengths to ensure that people are well equipped to address not only the challenges of today but also the challenges of the future. The central questions are as follows:

→ What is it your team will be accomplishing six months from now?

→ What specific results do you want/need to see?

→ How is that different from what your team is doing today?

→ What is needed to make these results happen?[15]

After answering these questions, each leader is responsible for addressing any talent gaps in his or her team. In many situations, this means bringing new members into the team with the necessary skills. This stands in contrast to other firms where the emphasis is on developing the existing members of the team through feedback, coaching, and mentoring. Netflix believes that team leaders often fool themselves into thinking that they can develop people who fundamentally lack the skills or temperament needed to be successful. Instead, it asks its managers to recognize when a person does not have the skills needed to be successful. The firm uses what it calls the "keeper test" to set a high standard in determining who stays and who goes. Managers are asked, at least once a year, to "testify" regarding which of their team members they would fight to keep if those people were considering leaving the company to go to other firms. Those whom the manager would not fight to keep should be asked to leave the company.[16]

The focus in Netflix is not on what you contributed in the past but on what you can contribute moving forward. The firm's loyalty is to the future, not the past. Those, for instance, who managed the growth of the Netflix DVD business may lack the skills needed to manage the growth of the firm's streaming business. Those who lead the streaming business may lack the skills needed to drive the production of original TV shows and movies. Those who built the U.S. business may lack the skills to manage the firm's expansion into international business. Netflix does not believe people should inherit future roles based on past achievements if they lack what is needed to drive future growth. To pay and retain people based on their past performance is bad for the performance of the business. It is also bad for the culture because it indicates, particularly to the new or younger people, that the company is not as performance driven as it claims. This management philosophy goes against the practices of many firms where past achievements are recognized by ensuring future roles within the company. Netflix is different. If you can't contribute to the firm's future growth, you are likely out of a job.

Managers, in general, can find reasons to avoid doing the painful work of removing those who are a poor fit to a company's future needs. This occurs for any number of reasons. First, assessing the capabilities of people is not always an easy endeavor. Truly poor performance is evident, but average performance is more difficult to assess given the range of factors that can influence how a person performs (such as the difficulty of the task, the availability of resources, or the cooperation of other groups within a firm). Second, most managers care about their team members as well as their families. Removing people from their jobs should not be an easy task, and for many leaders, it is the most painful part of their jobs. Third, most supervisors seek to avoid the legal entanglements that can occur when employees are fired or demoted. This is particularly true when there is no paper trail documenting the reasons for removing someone from his or her job (or in striving to justify why they would be a fit for future demands). Finally, many managers believe that they can coach their people to higher levels of performance—even though past supervisors have failed in doing so. They assume that they, unlike others, have what it takes to improve the performance of underperforming individuals.

Netflix strives to overcome these obstacles by taking a different approach, summarized in the provocative statement, "Adequate performance in Netflix results in a generous severance package."[17] The firm realizes that the goal of creating a high-talent-density organization requires an effective way to let go of those who don't meet its high standards. The challenge is to move out of the company those who don't fit the firm's needs in a manner that causes the least amount of damage to the employee, his or her manager, and the company. In an effort to be fair to those let go and to minimize the pain felt by managers who ask people to leave the firm, Netflix offers a generous severance package (which begins at four months of salary even for those who have just joined the firm and is often higher for those with longer tenure). The company also wants to avoid legal action from those let go and thus strives to part with them on terms that are as good as possible.[18] A former Netflix human resources leader, who played a key role in building the firm's unique culture, describes how the firm separates from those who fail to meet its standards:

> We want them [the employees] to keep their dignity . . . . In many companies, once I want you to leave, my job is to prove you're incompetent. I have to give you all the documentation and fire you for poor performance. It can take months. Here, I write a check. We exchange severance for a release. To make Netflix a great company, people have to be able to leverage it when they leave by subsequently getting good jobs.[19]

The goal for Netflix, and other cutting-edge firms, is to create a culture obsessed with results without creating a culture that is too harsh. What is the point at which a firm or team pushes too far on results and, in so doing, undermines the very outcome it so desires?

✄

Netflix, of course, is not unique in being obsessed with creating a culture that delivers results. *The New York Times* recently ran a controversial article profiling the online retailer Amazon.[20] In it, the *Times* lauds Amazon for its success in embracing bold ideas and investing in long-term growth initiatives. Over its history, Amazon has consistently sacrificed near-term profits to fund projects that in some cases take years or even decades to pay off—if at all. In so doing, the firm ignores the pressure from some on Wall Street who want to see it deliver greater profits today. The *Times* article also compliments Amazon for its culture of candor, where issues are openly debated and people are given ample opportunity to impact the business. But all is not well in Amazon, according to the *Times*.

The article focuses primarily on Amazon's cultural weaknesses.[21] The company is described as one where people work hard and long, to the point of sacrificing their health and family lives. After interviewing more than 100 current and former employees, the *Times* authors suggest that it is common for people at Amazon to work during the night, over weekends, and during vacations, answering emails and completing work assignments. The article further suggests that some employees, when taking sick or personal leaves, will come back early for fear of losing their jobs. The result is a higher level of stress than what is found in other firms.[22] A second element of the Amazon culture that draws attention is the extensive use of data to assess employee performance. For example, Amazon monitors its distribution employees at a level beyond what is found in most firms. It tags employees with electronic trackers that indicate the route they must follow as they fill orders within the company's huge multi-acre warehouses. These trackers also give target times for each task and measure if those targets are met.[23] The resulting pressure means that those who can't keep up or are "time thieves" are, in the words of one publication, "pushed harder and harder to work faster and faster until they were terminated, they quit or they got injured."[24]

The pressure employees of Amazon feel to perform at the highest level exists in conjunction with an emphasis on operating in a frugal manner—which is seen as important not only to provide customers with low-cost products but as a means to drive innovation. The company believes that people should not simply throw money at the challenges they face but, instead, should think creatively about alternative solutions that may end up being superior. In its statement of leadership principles, frugality is described as the ability to "accomplish more with less. Constraints breed resourcefulness, self-sufficiency and invention. There are no extra points for growing headcount, budget size or fixed expense."[25] That focus, while logical if not admirable, has resulted in some questionable decisions regarding the company's workforce. For instance, several years ago Amazon built a new distribution facility in Pennsylvania to process and ship online orders. The distribution center was built without air conditioning, saving the company hundreds of thousands of dollars in construction and operating costs. Problems arose when a heat wave hit the area soon after the facility was completed, resulting in difficult working conditions (with temperatures reportedly over 100 degrees inside the facility). Amazon responded by having an ambulance waiting outside, staffed with paramedics for employees who might suffer from heat exhaustion. A local hospital, where a few workers were taken, reported Amazon to federal workplace safety regulators. Several media outlets found out about the conditions at the facility and ran stories with headlines criticizing the firm for its treatment of employees.[26] Amazon responded by installing air conditioning at the Pennsylvania distribution center as well as at other locations across the country.

Amazon is further described by the *Times* as a highly political culture where employees compete for jobs and recognition—a place where some employees will undermine coworkers if it benefits them. Amazon is certainly not unique if politics plays a role in how people behave within the company. Many slow-moving and bureaucratic firms are plagued by politics. But some believe that Amazon has created a more Darwinian, even Orwellian, culture that actively pits people against one another. For instance, Amazon uses a feedback system where people can provide their views regarding the strengths and weaknesses of their coworkers. The *Times* interviews indicate that this feedback tool is used by some at Amazon to provide negative feedback on those they see as competitors.[27] In so doing, they increase their own standings within the firm. The picture painted by the *Times*, and a number of other publications, is of a company that uses a variety of techniques to get the most of out of its people.

More than 5,000 readers posted comments in response the *Times* article—the highest number in the paper's history. Amazon became the focus of an intense debate about its practices and, by implication, what will be or should be the future of the workplace. The reactions fell into one of two camps. Some suggested that the article was unfair in portraying Amazon in an overly negative light. They asked, what is wrong with expecting people to perform at a high level? What is wrong with measuring performance with hard data? What is wrong with spending money in a frugal manner while investing billions to drive long-term growth? They suggest that Amazon, on almost any measure, is one of the great success stories in the history of business. The firm has changed the face of retailing and is growing at a rate that most firms can only envy.[28] No firm today can match Amazon's ability to provide the best selection of products, at the lowest price, and with the fastest delivery. It is branching out into new innovative areas with some notable successes, such as cloud services. The firm has grown each year and now has nearly 240,000 employees, twice as large as Apple and four times as large as Google. The success of the firm's stock price also suggests that Amazon, at least as viewed by investors, is being built for long-term success.[29] It is now one of the 10 largest firms in the world in market value—far beyond the worth of its primary brick-and-mortar competitor Walmart.

Bezos realizes that his company's culture will not be a good fit for those who prefer a more laid-back environment, one with less aggressive goals and lower performance standards. He openly states that some people may not want to work in an intense environment comprised of driven people who are constantly striving to meet high expectations—their own as well as the firm's. He noted, "You can work long, hard, or smart, but at Amazon.com you can't choose two out of the three."[30] That said, Bezos stated that the *Times* article describes a company that he doesn't recognize—a firm for which he would not want to work. He argues that his firm's distinctive culture, built over several decades, is attractive to many who find it, in Bezos' words, "energizing and meaningful." Others in the technology industry, as well as current and former Amazon employees, also suggest that the *Times* portrayal is inaccurate and unfair. In fact, many believe that the "Amazon Way" should not be criticized but instead viewed as a model for other firms—showing how a modern company needs to operate.

Those in the opposing camp, equally vehement in their views, believe that Amazon has created a harsh corporate culture where people, no matter how well paid, are cogs in the firm's growth machine. Individuals, from the viewpoint of these critics, are brought into the company, worked hard, and then discarded once they burn out or stop providing what the company wants. A former executive at Amazon, who was with the firm for 10 years, recalled a colleague telling her, "If you're not good, Jeff will chew you up and spit you out. And if you're good, he will jump on your back and ride you into the ground."[31] The firm's critics find fault with Amazon pushing performance to the extreme, through a variety of management techniques designed to get the most out of people (such as using employee trackers in its distribution centers). They suggest that Amazon, which generally pays people very well, is attracting new workers because people are naive about the firm's culture or because a poor economy forces them into jobs they would not take in more favorable times. In short, they view Amazon as a highly successful twenty-first-century sweatshop.

N

In the introduction, I outlined five practices of cutting-edge teams (such as fostering a collective obsession and valuing fit over experience). These practices focus on *how* these teams operate—their particular ways of thinking and behaving. But Amazon and Netflix call into question *what* firms and their teams need to achieve.[32] Defining what constitutes an ideal team outcome is not the same as how teams go about achieving those outcomes. Amazon, in particular, is a fascinating company because it calls into question people's beliefs regarding the definition of success. Few can deny that Amazon is an extraordinary company on almost any financial, operational, or customer metric. That may be enough for most people—especially its shareholders. The key question, then, is, does a company need to deliver anything beyond results? More specifically, how do we define success for a company and team? What do companies and teams need to achieve, if anything, beyond results? When does the push for results become too extreme and self-defeating?

Let's start by defining results. Broadly stated, *results* means that a team delivers what is expected of it by those who benefit from its products and services.[33] This is often seen as a team meeting the expectations of its customers or clients. But for many teams, this means meeting the expectations of the organizations for which they work (and, specifically, meeting the expectations of the leaders who run their organizations). These goals can involve financial targets (such as monthly sales), as well as growth targets (such as the percentage of customers using a firm's products). Amazon, for instance, started a new business providing cloud storage, seeing it as an opportunity to grow outside of its core retailing business. That business is now one of the firm's fastest growing and most profitable groups, and it may one day exceed Amazon's retail business in revenues (as it already does in profit). The team responsible for developing this business has clearly delivered results for customers who value the service it provides. The team has also produced results for the company and its shareholders.

Viewing results only in terms of financial outcomes, however, is too limited. In some cases, teams work toward goals beyond, or even in conflict with, revenue and profit. For example, the clothing company Patagonia decided several years ago that it would use organic cotton in its clothing. This was done because producing organic cotton causes less damage to the environment than conventionally grown cotton. Customers were not asking for this change, but the leaders of Patagonia saw it as part of the firm's environmental mission to extract less of a toll on the planet in the running of its business. As a result, a team within Patagonia was tasked with shifting the company to organic cotton even though the cost of doing so would be significant. This was no simple endeavor, as few suppliers at the time were producing organic cotton. However, the commitment of the company to the environment was so central that it worked with growers to produce organic cotton. Patagonia's founder noted,

> Switching over to organically grown cotton was a really big deal. Once I found out that cotton was the most damaging fiber that we could make clothing out of, I gave the company 18 months to completely get out of making any product with industrially grown cotton. But you can't just call the fabric supplier and say, "Give me 10,000 yards of organic shirting." We had to revolutionize the industry.[34]

Results, then, are much more than simply achieving financial targets—cutting-edge teams achieve results that move their firms closer to their stated reason for being. Achieving results for Patagonia in regard to organic cotton was not simply maximizing revenue or profit. Nor was the goal to gain a marketing advantage in being viewed as an environmentally friendly company (although that was one outcome). Results, in this case, meant taking action consistent with the core mission of Patagonia. Whole Foods is similar to Patagonia in viewing its mission as being more important than the achievement of near-term financial goals. Whole Foods, of course, does measure and reward financial performance. It also maintains that profit is necessary and good in allowing it to broaden the firm's impact in helping people live better and healthier lives. However, the firm's leaders believe that an excessive focus on financial performance often results in bad decisions that don't lead to good outcomes over the long term. The goal, according to the Whole Foods CEO, is to take the right action for the right reasons—which are actions that advance the higher purpose of the firm.[35]

A final point on results. The need to produce results includes building the organizational capabilities required to deliver those results. In other words, delivering results means that firms and teams develop the skills to deliver what is needed not just next month or next quarter but over the long term. This starts with enhancing the capabilities of the individual members of each team. In some cases, the focus is on developing the skills of existing team members through challenging assignments, training, and coaching. In other cases, such as at Netflix, it means bringing in people with the talent that the firm needs. Capability development also means that companies improve their ability to support their teams. They develop formal and informal processes that their teams need to be successful. Pixar, for example, has created a host of team-friendly practices, such as providing detailed feedback to a film crew as its project progresses. Delivering results, then, is not just delivering on expectations in the short term—it requires continuous improvements in the capabilities of those on the team, the way the team functions as a group, and the environment in which it operates.

For many hard-edge business people, teams exist only to produce results. Other factors are important to the extent that they support or hinder a team's ability to achieve a desired outcome. In particular, the relationships among team members either enable results when a team "gels" or, on the other extreme, hinder results when factions within the group undermine its ability to operate at a high level. Relationships, from this point of view, are a means to an end—and are not on par with the need to deliver results. The chief designer at Apple, Jony Ives, tells a story about Steve Jobs that illustrates this point.[36] Jobs believed that a key to his success was staffing his teams with highly talented people. His role as a leader was then to push them to achieve more than they thought possible. At one point, Jobs was unhappy with the product that Ives and his team were developing. Consistent with his reputation, Jobs was tough on the team in pointing out the product's flaws. Ives went to Jobs after the team review and suggested a less aggressive approach in giving feedback to his team. Jobs asked why he should soften his approach and be less direct, given the glaring problems with the product. Ives said it was because he didn't want to undermine the group's morale. He described the resulting interaction between Jobs and himself:

> I remember asking him why it could have been perceived in his critique of a piece of work [that] he was a little bit too harsh. We'd been putting our heart and soul into this. I said, couldn't we . . . moderate the things we said? And he said, "Well, why?" And I said, "Because I care about the team." And he said this brutally brilliantly insightful thing, what he said was, "No Jony, you're just really vain." . . . . "No, you just want people to like you. And I'm surprised at you because I thought you really held the work up as the most important, not how you believed you were perceived by other people." And I was terribly cross because I knew he was right.[37]

Ives told this story out of respect for Jobs' ability to focus on what was needed to deliver a great product—in particular, his commitment to giving clear, unambiguous, and tough feedback. But, at the same time, Ives stated that his own greatest achievement at Apple was not the creation of the iPhone or any other Apple product. Instead, he was most proud of his design team and its work process. He noted that no one had left his group voluntarily during his tenure. Ives was suggesting that Jobs was both right and wrong in his view of how teams need to operate. Jobs felt that leaders should care only for the quality of the product or service being produced regardless of the feelings of team members (particularly the feelings of team members toward the team leader). Ives, however, feels that the relationships among members are a critical element in producing great results and need to be nurtured accordingly.

✎

Robert Putnam, a sociologist, is the author of *Bowling Alone*. In the book, he describes the central role of interpersonal bonds in a society and the forces that are making such bonds less common.[38] He uses the term *social capital* to describe how these relationships operate in a variety of settings, including nonprofit, public, and private organizations. Social capital, in the simplest terms, is the "glue" that connects people together and, in so doing, helps groups, organizations, and society function more effectively. In particular, social capital plays a role in encouraging individuals to support others for reasons other than their self-interest. An example that Putnam highlights is the willingness of people to give their money and time to community food banks. No one forces people to support community organizations, but many do so willingly. In the private sector, Putnam describes another form of social capital in the networks that exist among various companies and leaders in Silicon Valley. These informal networks produce, in some cases, voluntary cooperation among people and companies, which in turn facilitates the development of new technologies. The central premise of Putnam's book is that interpersonal connections are critical to the health of a society and the success of its various institutions.

A related aspect of social capital is the idea that it is an asset that can be accumulated and then used when needed. For instance, the social capital that has developed within a team can help it withstand the setbacks that occur as it goes about its work—as the relationships among team members produce greater commitment to each other's success and the success of the group. In contrast, teams lacking in social capital are more likely to fail when facing adversity, as relationships among members are inadequate or even negative, compromising the ability of the group to work toward an effective solution. Social capital, of course, does not guarantee a group's success, as myriad factors influence performance. But it increases the likelihood of success within a team or firm.[39]

A vivid illustration of the role played by social capital is found among soldiers on a battlefield. Countries fight wars for many reasons, but soldiers fight primarily for each other. That is, they fight to support the survival of those they interact with every day, versus fighting for an abstract cause such as democracy or freedom or even against a common enemy. The closer the ties among a group of soldiers, the more likely they are to put themselves in harm's way for each other.[40] An analysis of soldier behavior in the Civil War tested this assumption. The researchers Dora Costa and Matthew Kahn sought to determine why more men did not desert on the battlefront. They examined data on the composition of various army units and their desertion rates. The researchers found that a range of factors impacted the willingness of soldiers to fight. But the key was having a closely bound company, in which soldiers shared much in common. That was the single most significant factor in determining a soldier's loyalty and willingness to fight. They write, "Was it their commitment to the cause, having the 'right stuff' high morale officers, or comrades? After examining all these explanations, we find that loyalty to comrades trumped cause, morale and leadership."[41] Their findings suggest that social capital is critically important when seeking to understand the thinking and behavior of soldiers under the most stressful of situations.

Research from the battlefront, particularly from a war fought over 150 years ago, may seem like a stretch in explaining how teams operate in modern corporations. But consider the findings of the Gallup organization in its study of effective organizations. Gallup research indicates that the level of employee engagement in a workgroup, which is the degree to which people are committed to their team and engaged in their work, is highly correlated to the degree to which they believe they have a best friend at work.[42] People who indicated that they have a best friend at work were, in general, more positive about their work and their company. The Gallup research found, for example, that those who report having a best friend at work were

→ 43 percent more likely (than average) to report having received praise or recognition for their work in the past seven days

→ 27 percent more likely to report that the mission of their company makes them feel their jobs are important

→ 27 percent more likely to report that their opinions seem to count at work

→ 21 percent more likely to report that at work, they have the opportunity to do what they do best every day

At face value, these appear to be absurd findings, particularly when one is seeking to determine the factors that allow a company or team to perform at a high level. As a consultant, I have worked with leaders who receive survey feedback from Gallup and ask, "How does having a best friend impact how my people view the mission of the company or the degree to which their opinions matter at work? Are we running a company or organizing a high-school social?" But these findings make sense if we think of having a best friend at work as an indicator of the strength of social capital within a group. Higher levels of social capital have a positive impact on the general behavior and perceptions of people within a team or organization. In settings with high levels of social capital, people are connected not just by what they think about their company and its leaders— but also by the connections they have at work.[43]

✴

Putnam, in *Bowling Alone*, suggests there are two types of social capital. *Bonding* is the connection among members within the same group. Examples include the Whole Foods in-store teams or the Pixar teams working on a film. *Building*, in contrast, is the connection among people who work in different groups. In this case, people cross group boundaries and collaborate with those in other groups. The members of a product development team, for example, need to work closely with members of a manufacturing team within a company to produce a successful product. A more specific example is found at Pixar, which views collaboration among various groups within the company as essential to the success of a film. The firm has a norm that anyone can talk to anyone else in the company without going through the formal chain of command (which is the norm in many companies). Its belief in the value of interconnectedness even takes on some humorous elements. I was told by an individual who worked for Pixar that people use an expression that underscores how important it is to connect with others: "Good hallway" means that you engage people as you pass them walking through the Pixar headquarters building—you say hello, chat briefly, or at least nod in recognition. He noted, "It is our way of saying that it is important to acknowledge others and help build the community. It also indicates that you are not meek and will reach out to others. Pixar as a company believes in cross-pollination and connecting with others is important to our success."

Putnam argues that both bonding and building are needed to produce a sufficient level of social capital within a society or group. We can add a third type of social capital—*believing*. This is the connection that people have to the organization that employs them. It is based on the belief that their organization is doing the right things and is worthy of their commitment. This is a connection beyond those within one's own team and even with those in other teams. It is an emotional investment in the company and its leaders. Social capital, then, consists of three types of relationships:

➡ *Bonding* **with Fellow Team Members:** Sustaining relationships involves a range of people-oriented elements of group life, with the most important being the relationships among team members. This includes the ability of team members to gel and produce something greater than the team members could produce working alone. This is not, however, about people simply liking each other.

Instead, it involves feeling connected to a group of people who share a common goal.[44]

➡ *Building* **Partnerships with Other Teams:** Relationships also require that team members work productively with other teams. Note that this involves more than simply being aware of those in other groups—it requires a more personal awareness and investment in the relationship. Much of the literature on teams focuses on the relationships among team members, but the level of relationships with those in other teams is often as important to the group's success.

➡ *Believing* **in One's Company and its Leaders:** This is the connection that people have with their organization—and, in the most positive cases, a belief that their company and its leaders share their values and beliefs. This results in an emotional investment in the firm and its reason for being.

Types of Social Capital

To illustrate the role of social capital, consider a team that is developing a new product—let's say a new smartphone. The new product draws widespread praise and meets its initial sales targets. However, factions developed within the team resulting in a high level of distrust among its members. This made it difficult for some members of the team to work together after the launch of its new product. The team also worked in a highly insular manner, alienating other teams within the company whom they saw as competing for resources and leadership support. The team withheld information from other teams and hoarded resources to maximize its own success. The product development team came to view its company as being led by "corporate suits" who didn't understand their product or provide the support it needed. Team members felt that they achieved success in spite of the obstacles placed in their way by the company and its leadership. As a result of these factors, the product development team disbanded after the launch, with some members even leaving the company. In this example, the team achieved results on one level but failed to develop social capital needed for the team to sustain its success over time.

Social capital is typically viewed as less important than the achievement of results (at least in a business setting). There are several reasons this occurs. First, survival is job one for organizations, and they depend on their teams to deliver. Motorola, for example, sold a popular cellphone called the RAZR but needed a new generation of smartphones that could compete with the products being offered by its rivals. The next-generation Motorola phone arrived late and without the features it needed to be successful.[45] Blame for that outcome goes to the design team responsible for the phone as well as the larger Motorola organization, which failed to provide the guidance and support the team needed. The firm never recovered and was eventually sold to Google. Second, results are typically defined by clear metrics that are in most cases easy to monitor (such as sales or profit). Social capital, in contrast, is fuzzy and hard to measure. Third, results in most organizations are tied to rewards of various types while the quality of the relationships within a team may be recognized but not rewarded. For example, teams that launch a successful product are rewarded financially and otherwise. In contrast, teams that fail to build social capital are typically not held accountable, particularly if they deliver the product. Fourth, efforts to manage relationships within a group or team add complexity to the challenges already facing a team and its leader. This is the case because team members have different motives, styles of operating, and, in particular, ways of dealing with stress and conflict. Relationships, then, are not only difficult to measure but difficult to manage. Even when a leader believes relationships are important, determining how to foster productive relationships is a challenge. For example, what is a leader to do if he or she gets Gallup survey results that indicate that people on his or her team don't trust each other? Many team leaders, unsure of what to do, resort to superficial team-building events and exercises. Finally, some leaders believe relationships get in the way of making tough calls on people and projects when needed. From this viewpoint, the personal connections in a team have a negative downside in preventing leaders, and others, from being as direct as needed (particularly when a team member is underperforming). In these situations, people can come to value harmonious relationships more than the achievement of results. An example of this is a team leader I know who is good at managing his team members until he has worked with them for a while—then he is less objective in how he views them and, in particular, their performance—and less willing to move them if they are underperforming.

Relationships are important because in the best situations they enable results. This is the Pixar experience, where the ability of team members to work collaboratively is critical to a film's success. Positive relationships within a team or company can also be an asset in attracting and retaining a talented workforce (as most people want to work in a company culture that is challenging but also supportive). There is, however, a more basic argument regarding the need for strong relationships within organizations and teams. The history of industry shows us that practices that were once voluntary (such as a 40-hour work week, safe working conditions, and minimum wages) are now mandatory. These changes were not made because they enhanced results. In fact, many if not most were resisted by a significant number of people in the business community because they added costs. Many firms complied because they were forced to do so as a result of legislation or because they wanted to conform with emerging social norms. The opportunity for people to connect with others in groups of various types is a basic human need. People want to be a part of communities where they form bonds with others. The opposite, in the more extreme form, is social isolation—which extracts a heavy toll.[46] Beyond one's family, the workplace is now the most important environment for many people—and for some, their workplaces are even more important than their families. Many people spend more of their waking hours at work than at home. Providing people with a work environment that meets their relationship needs may become an obligation that, while not mandated, is expected. In contrast, the controversy surrounding Amazon's culture results from what some argue is a punishing or even hostile work environment. Providing people with a sense of community is not typically described as a goal in itself—but perhaps that will be the case in the future. Is it unreasonable to assume that more companies will come to believe, like Whole Foods or Zappos, that they have obligations to provide individuals with work environments that enhance their lives and, in particular, provides them with a sense of community? This is not, of course, meant to suggest that relationships come at the expense of results. It is, however, meant to propose that relationships at work will increasingly be more than a means to an end.

The results/relationship model of team life is supported by a number of studies that examine social perceptions. In one group of studies, researchers found that people assess others based on two primary dimensions: competence and warmth. People with the skills and drive needed to achieve a desired outcome are deemed to be competent. People who are supportive of others and helpful are deemed to be warm. These two factors are "the basic dimensions that, together, account almost entirely for how people characterize others."[47] Those who want to be viewed positively by others must be both warm and competent (or at least viewed as such). Moreover, the researchers found that the perception of another's warmth appears to be the first criteria in judging them—as people assess the intentions of others (their warmth) before determining their ability to carry through with those intentions (their competence). While the researchers don't make this leap, we can assume that teams are viewed in a similar manner by their members. First, people assess if their team is a warm place to work, one with positive relationships, where others will be helpful and supportive. Second, does the team have the capabilities needed to deliver results and be successful?

An unrelated study by Teresa Amabile and her colleagues focused on the factors that enable high performance in organizations, with a particular interest on the role of helping behavior.[48] The researchers asked people in the design company IDEO to identify colleagues who helped them in their work and then rate these individuals on three attributes—their competence (ability to perform a job at a high level), trustworthiness (someone that others feel comfortable sharing their thoughts and feelings with), and accessibility (in being available to those who need help). The researchers also asked people to rate randomly selected colleagues who didn't make their "helper" list. They found, overall, that the highest rated helpers were also those highest in perceived trustworthiness and accessibility. Competence, of course, mattered—it was higher in those viewed as being helpful in comparison to nonhelpers. But competence was not the driving force in who was rated as most helpful. Those who were seen as supportive (in this case, trustworthy and accessible) were viewed as being the most helpful in solving the challenges facing their colleagues.

Results and Relationships = Team Success

Results	Relationships
Current Results: The team delivers on the expectations of its customers/clients	**Bonding:** The team develops necessary cohesion among its members
Future Results: The team builds the capabilities needed to deliver results in the future	**Building:** The team collaborates with other teams in the organization
	Believing: The team identifies with the organization in which it works

Results and relationships, then, are the two essential outcomes that firms and their teams need to achieve.[49] But more is not always better. Both results and relationships have potential downsides. For example, a singular and relentless emphasis on results can undermine a team and its performance. This occurs for several reasons. First, a results-obsessed culture can wear out the individuals on a team. The Pixar *Toy Story* case is an example of pushing results to the point where it becomes destructive to individuals and a team. An excessive drive to deliver can come from the senior leaders of a company, from a team's leader, or from the team members themselves. In many cases, it is a combination of all three factors. The challenge is delivering results without creating a culture that is too harsh—a culture where people compete with each other in unproductive ways or live in constant fear of losing their jobs. Take the case of Tony Fadell, who was a highly successful executive at Apple before starting the firm Nest Labs (which produces "smart" thermostats, smoke detectors, and security systems). Fadell has a reputation of pushing himself and his people hard—and he delivered at Apple and initially at his own firm.[50] Then things started to unravel. One sign of the problems at the company involved the failed integration of

Dropcam, a video camera and cloud-computing company that Nest bought in 2014. In short order, one-half of the 100 Dropcam employees who came to Nest with the acquisition resigned. The founder of Dropcam said that Nest, and Fadell in particular, crushed his group's ability to build great products. His critics described Fadell's management style as highly aggressive and controlling—to the point of alienating many of those responsible for developing his firm's new products.[51] Fadell, however, has no regrets. He proudly notes that his leadership style is one of "holding people to a higher standard than they thought they could achieve and pushing them beyond what they thought they could achieve."[52]

An excessive emphasis on results can also embolden people to cross ethical and legal boundaries. That is, there are some who will cut corners or even break the law in a desire to produce results for themselves and their company. They do this for self-serving reasons (they reap the financial and career benefits of meeting their goals) and because of pressure from the top of the company (they fear being fired if they fail to deliver). The recent Volkswagen (VW) scandal appears to be an example of this dynamic. Emissions tests were deliberately rigged by staff in the firm's engineering group to deliver on VW's aggressive sales targets—which were part of a larger strategy to make the automaker the largest in the world. VW, as a result, installed stealth software in its diesel cars that created false emissions readings. This allowed the company to market cars that performed well for customers while appearing to meet regulatory requirements. The company's deception, undetected for years, has resulted in the largest class-action settlement in history (totaling more than $14.7 billion in the United States alone). As with many organization failures, the culprit appears to be the culture of the company. VW is a tough, some would say arrogant, firm where mandates are issued from the top and those in middle-management positions feel they have no choice but to find a way to meet those expectations. The diesel engineers didn't have a way to meet the requirements of their senior leaders, so they developed an unethical workaround. The company fired the engineers who committed the fraud, and a number of senior leaders, including the CEO, have resigned or been fired. The question remains, however, whether the culture of the firm will fundamentally change as a result of this scandal.[53]

A second case of results being pushed too far involves the pharmaceutical company Valeant. The company is currently in turmoil as a result of questionable distributor practices and financial reporting. Its stock has imploded, and various regulatory groups, including the U.S. Senate, are examining how it operates. The firm has hired a new CEO and is reviewing its business practices. In a press release announcing these changes, it noted, "The company has determined that the tone at the top of the organization and the performance-based environment at the company, where challenging targets were set and achieving those targets was a key performance expectation, may have been contributing factors resulting in the company's improper revenue recognition."[54] VW and Valeant are not unique. In any given month, one can find stories in the *Wall Street Journal* about a company, or more often about a team within a company, acting in unethical ways to enhance financial results. The founder of the Chinese Internet commerce company Alibaba, Jack Ma, describes this as a "wild dog" culture where people use dishonest means to gain an advantage for their firms. In an interview, he noted that these companies have an inherent weakness: "Yes, it's true they make more money, but the money is from dishonest dealings, and may cost the company in the long run. When that generation becomes company leaders, the company will be weak because they get used to being dishonest and taking advantages."[55] Relationships, like results, can also be pushed too far. In particular, strong interpersonal bonds among teammates can lead to increasingly negative outcomes for a team. The first potential downside of overly cohesive groups is that members are prone to groupthink. Research indicates that teams of people who are close interpersonally are more likely to converge in their thinking and more limited in considering alternatives in addressing the challenges they face.

Also, they are more likely to be overconfident in their course of action and less inclined to fully appreciate the risks they face moving forward.[56] A related downside of an overly cohesive group is the avoidance of tough or contentious issues within the group.[57] One study, for example, examined the relationship between social ties and performance in a group of travel agents. The researchers found that interpersonal relationships among the travel agents, when taken too far, eroded a team's performance. This was determined by examining the ties among workers based on the frequency of their email exchanges over a period of one year. The strength of the interpersonal ties was then correlated to the sales results of each team. The findings indicate that the teams with very little social cohesion had lower performance than average groups. This is not surprising, as there was little bonding among the members (which would have helped enhance their collective learning and performance). But the most interesting finding of the study was that stronger interpersonal ties increased team performance only to a certain point, and then performance began to decline. The researchers suggest that social ties, if very strong, can become more time consuming and important than the performance of the team.

Close interpersonal bonds can also result in people being overly protective of those in their own group, even when they act in inappropriate or unethical ways. Myriad studies suggest that loyalty to the group has a strong impact on people's willingness to surface unpleasant truths and even unethical acts. In these situations, loyalty to the team becomes more important than dealing with problems or concerns. In case after case, some team members don't come forward with concerns because they want to be accepted by their group. An overly cohesive group, then, increases the possibility that members are less likely to confront tough issues that, once surfaced, would disrupt the social relations within the group or result in others perceiving "truth-telling" individuals as being disloyal to the team.[58]

Another liability of close interpersonal bonds is the creation of in-groups and out-groups. Teams with tight bonds can develop an in-group mentality that, to varying degrees, excludes others. Those excluded may be people within the team who are seen as less capable or important. An in-group mentality can also impact how team members interact with those in other groups, whose support is often needed for a team to be successful. The bonds among team members can become so strong that they result in viewing others as outsiders who are not to be trusted. Take, for example, the experience of a past CFO at the clothing company Patagonia. He reported that he came to feel like an outcast within his new company because he didn't have the history and close interpersonal connections that existed among the firm's other senior leaders. This condition was compounded by the fact that he didn't live in the same neighborhood or socialize outside of work with his senior-level peers. "I liked my work, but my personal life was separate," he recalls. "There was a lot of pressure to be a Patagoniac. I hated that term, and I hated the concept." Failing to develop a close relationship with those running the company, he eventually departed.[59]

Finally, an overemphasis on relationships can result in emotional overload. Research indicates that people, in general, have a limited supply of empathy, and a relationship-focused culture will place more demands on connecting with others. An emphasis on relationships can result in what some call "compassion fatigue," where a great deal of energy is expended in building and maintaining relationships.[60] Research further suggests that organizations can place an unequal burden on women in the area of relationship management. This occurs because women, based on social norms, are viewed by many as being more communal and caring than men. As a result, they are expected, although it may never be stated as such, to do more of the work of building and sustaining relationships at work. Some refer to this, when it impacts the workplace, as emotional labor. This work requires taking the time to ensure that people connect with one another and do what is needed to ensure that the work environment fosters collaboration. The end result can be that women, particularly if relationships are emphasized within a company, become burdened more than men in building relationships. Logic suggests that both and men and women would be equally engaged in relationship building at work—the reality, however, may be otherwise. The downside for women is that they may be expected to do relationship work that is time consuming and often unrecognized.[61] In one study, for example, scholars Madeline E. Heilman and Julie Chen found that women were rated more harshly if they didn't help another, in contrast to their male counterparts. They also received less "credit" when they did help a colleague—in part because they were expected to do so. Adam Grant and Sheryl Sandberg, commenting on this study, note, "Over and over, after giving identical help, a man was significantly more likely to be recommended for promotions, important projects, raises and bonuses. A woman had to help just to get the same rating as a man who didn't help."[62]

The Logic and Limits of Results and Relationships

The Need for Results

- Team meets the current expectations of the organization and customers
- Team builds the capabilities needed to deliver results in the future

The Need for Relationships

- Cohesion among team members
- Collaboration with other teams
- Belief in the company and its leaders

The Risks of Excessive Results

Increased potential for . . .

- Burnout of team members
- Bruising organizational culture
- A results-at-any-cost mentality

The Risks of Excessive Relationships

Increased potential for . . .

- Team groupthink
- Avoidance of tough issues
- In-group/out-group dynamics

✎

Teams face two essential risks in managing the results/relation-ships polarity. The first is that a team will push either results or relationships too far and suffer the consequences of being too extreme. This sometimes occurs because of what some describe as an "either/or mentality" in a team or its leaders.[63] In this case, a team views either results or relationships as the primary or only goal and, as a result, pays insufficient attention to the other side of the polarity. There are teams that act with a "results only matter" mentality and teams that act with a "relationships only matter" mentality. One goal of recognizing the importance of both is to de-termine how each can be pursued in the most effective manner. There is no cookbook or step-by-step formula that can be followed to deliver results and build relationships. Take, for instance, the process of removing those who are underperforming. A company may work very hard to hire the most capable people and give them everything they need to be successful (training, peer support, feed-back, ...). But there are inevitably cases where mistakes are made and people don't have the drive or skill needed to perform at the highest level. However, removing these people is difficult in a cul-ture that emphasizes relationships. An Airbnb employee noted,

> We have a community culture, a "we all get along" culture, which is unique and powerful. Airbnb is the most people-cen-tered company I have seen over my career in the tech industry. However, one problem with our culture is that poor performers are often allowed to stay in the firm. They are transferred to another group or given a less important job. This occurs be-cause managers don't want to be seen as someone who fires people. Managers know what is going on with their poor per-formers but will not take action. This hurts the morale of those who are working hard and having an impact.[64]

Other firms, such as Netflix, move quickly in making the tough call on those who can't deliver what is needed. These companies believe that successful firms often stumble and in some cases fail because they avoid facing the reality that their talent levels are below what they need to win in a competitive marketplace. You might assume, then, that the best approach is to act decisively when talent gaps are identified within a group. However, Pixar takes a different view. It believes that acting too quickly creates unproductive fear within the workplace, as people are wondering if they will be next to be fired. This distracts people from the work and, in particular, undermines their creativity. Pixar believes a company is better served by waiting until the need to remove an underperformer, even when that person is the team's leader, is recognized by everyone on the team. At Pixar, this often means removing a director from a film whose team has already come to the conclusion that the director must go. Then the decision to re-move the director is supported without creating undue anxiety.[65] You might assume, then, that it is best to wait a bit longer than needed to remove underperforming talent. The best time to re-move talent depends on a number of factors, and each approach has its own risk. Some leaders move too quickly and create un-productive anxiety in those who remain on the team. Some lead-ers move too slowly and put the team at risk. Each leader needs to weigh these considerations and determine, given the work to be done and the nature of the team, the proper timing and ap-proach to making necessary changes.

The opposite risk, which I find more prevalent as a management consultant, is that many teams do not push results and relation-ships far enough and, as a result, fail to achieve what is needed for them to grow. This occurs in some cases because teams strive to manage the results and relationships dilemma by maintaining an acceptable balance between the two—avoiding extremes in either area. That is, they strive to achieve enough results *and* enough re-lationships to be successful (or at least avoid failure) but not so much that it creates problems.[66] This tactic, while understandable, can result in an equilibrium trap. In this situation, the team strives to maintain a steady state between results and relationships despite challenges that require it to move beyond the status quo in how it manages one or both. Teams in this situation strive for stability and predictability in a world that is often unstable and highly competitive.

Cutting-edge teams avoid falling into the equilibrium trap by pushing both results and relationships to the extreme. Then they manage the very real downsides of doing so. Progress requires moving between these two extremes, sometimes simultaneously, but often in one direction and then the other, depending on the conditions that exist and the needs of the team. In either case, the team acts, for some period of time, as if only results matter or as if only relationships matter. In essence, they ask, "What actions would we take as a team if only results mattered?" Or, on the other extreme, they ask, "What actions would we take if only relationships mattered?" The outcome is a productive dialectic—a constant and healthy tension between results and relationships within a team. The leaders of these teams recognize that one side of the polarity can't be pursued for long in the absence of the other. Progress, however, is not achieved by being less aggressive in each area. Instead, it is made by pushing both results and relationships to the breaking point.

Pushing the extremes, when done skillfully, creates virtuous or upward cycles in teams. These are situations where achieving results in a team enhances relationships and, in turn, where relationships enhance results. This is the opposite of destructive or downward cycles, where a decline in a team's results undermines relationships, which become strained as the pressure mounts to turn around the team's performance. There are also situations where relationships deteriorate to a point of undermining the ability of the team to produce results. The goal, of course, is to create virtuous team cycles where results and relationships operate in a manner to produce ever higher levels of team performance.

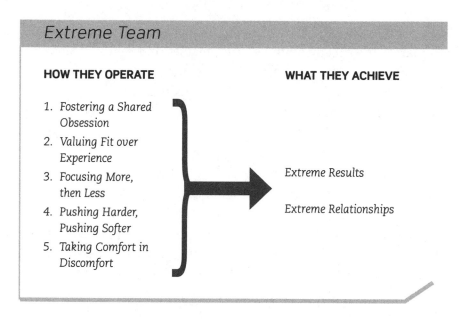

Extreme Team

HOW THEY OPERATE

1. *Fostering a Shared Obsession*
2. *Valuing Fit over Experience*
3. *Focusing More, then Less*
4. *Pushing Harder, Pushing Softer*
5. *Taking Comfort in Discomfort*

WHAT THEY ACHIEVE

Extreme Results

Extreme Relationships

 *TAKEAWAYS*

> ➤ The fundamental dynamic in teams is delivering results while building relationships. Every team faces the challenge of doing both.

> ➤ In many cases, results and relationships are synergistic— each supporting the other and producing virtuous cycles (where results enhance relationships and relationships enhance results).

> ➤ In some situations, however, results and relationships are antagonistic, with extremes in one undermining the other. An excessive focus on results can erode relationships; an excessive focus on relationships can erode results.

➤ Many teams strive to manage the interplay between results and relationships by maintaining an acceptable equilibrium—enough results and enough relationships to move the group forward without taking undue risk.

➤ Striving for equilibrium, however, is a seductive trap. It can result in stagnation as a team seeks to maintain a comfortable balance between results and relationships in an environment that requires more of each.

➤ Genius, in teams, is found at the edges. Cutting-edge teams push results and relationships to the breaking point with an understanding of the need to manage the risks that come with doing so.

FOSTER A SHARED OBSESSION

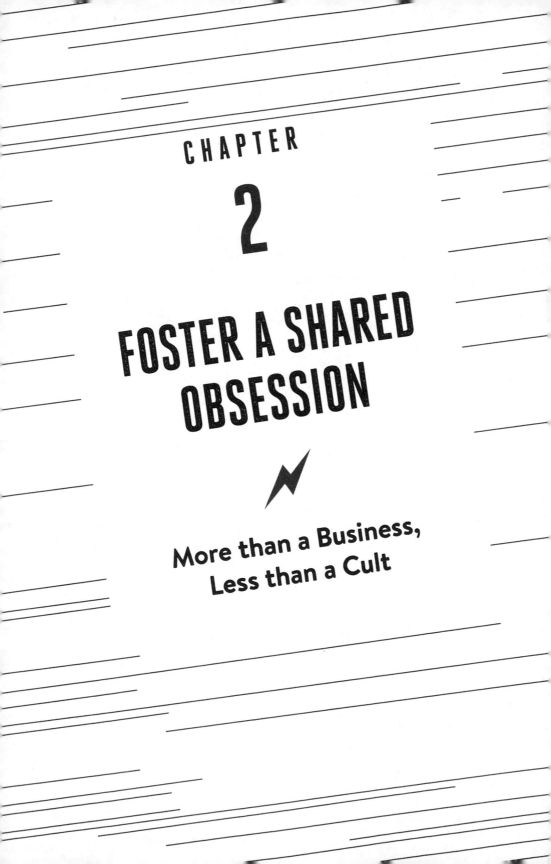

More than a Business, Less than a Cult

The founder of Patagonia, Yvon Chouinard, is a man of strong convictions. He openly declares, for example, his preference for some customers over others. He favors those he fondly calls "dirt bags"—people, like himself, who engage in high-intensity outdoor activities such as rock climbing, whitewater kayaking, and surfing.[1] They push themselves to the extremes and take full advantage of how his firm's products perform under demanding conditions. They also care about the environment and do their part to protect it. Chouinard is equally direct in expressing his disdain for those who wear his clothing as fashion statements while running errands in gas-guzzling Range Rovers.[2] When asked if his views might alienate some of his most loyal customers, he says,

> I couldn't care less. I could get 10,000 letters saying "Take me off your mailing list" and it wouldn't bother me . . . . What they don't realize is that I'm not in the business to make clothes. I'm not in the business to make more money for myself, for Christ's sake. This is the reason Patagonia exists—to put into action the recommendations I read about in books to avoid environmental collapse. I'm in business—to try to clean up our own act, and try to influence other companies to do the right thing, and try to influence our customers to do the right thing. So we're not going to change. They can go buy from somewhere else if they don't like it.[3]

Chouinard doesn't see himself as a businessman. In fact, he hates the term. He is an environmentalist who built a $750 million company.[4] His disregard for common business practices has resulted in some missteps along with way—including a near-death experience for the company several decades ago.[5] Chouinard admits that Patagonia made some classic blunders. The firm at one time had an unwieldy organizational structure, poor inventory management processes, and little or no training for its new managers. The firm also suffered, early in its history, with significant turnover at the senior levels—people, in Chouinard's view, who didn't fit the firm's culture. Some of those who departed had a different view—suggesting that Chouinard was a difficult and divisive boss. Others view Yvon as a highly idiosyncratic leader but one whom they trust. One noted, "Yvon is an interesting leader in that he is not particularly charismatic. He is passionate about what he believes but can, at times, be cynical and introverted. He is, however, the most authentic leader I have seen over my career. There is no BS and no backing down from what he believes is right."[6]

Patagonia survived, learned from its mistakes, and became an iconic clothing brand. Over the years, Chouinard has ignored offers to buy Patagonia. He also refused to take his company public regardless of the financial windfall that he and his family would realize in doing so. Keeping Patagonia private gives him more freedom to run the company as he sees fit. No shareholders pressuring him to grow faster. No quarterly earnings call to explain his investments and donations. No analyst asking questions about profit margins.

Chouinard has dedicated his life to reducing the harm that individuals, and companies, have on the planet. Patagonia is his primary means of achieving that goal—starting with his firm's charitable support of environmental causes. Each year, Patagonia donates 1 percent of its annual revenue to conservation groups. Patagonia also gives employees time off, up to two months with pay, to work on environmental efforts. One employee, for example, tracked the movement of wolves in Yellowstone National Park in an effort to enhance their survival and, in so doing, help maintain a healthy balance in the park's ecosystem. Patagonia also strives to be a good corporate role model, inspiring other firms as well as its customers to live in a planet-friendly way.[7] Chouinard's focus on the environment has resulted in a unique corporate culture and, at times, some surprising actions. Perhaps the most notable occurred when the company ran an advertisement asking people not to buy its clothing (with the headline "Don't Buy this Jacket" placed above a photograph of a popular Patagonia jacket). The ad's subtext stated that to lighten their environmental impact, people need to consume less and companies needed to make less. It may be the first time in history that a business asked people not to buy its products.[8]

Causing no unnecessary harm to the environment is one of two key priorities at Patagonia. Making the best possible product is the other. The importance of quality was evident early in the firm's history. The precursor of Patagonia was little more than a blacksmith shop operating out of a garage. Chouinard made climbing hardware for a small circle of his friends, all outdoor enthusiasts. The goal was to make equipment that was stronger, lighter, and more reliable than competitive products. Chouinard wrote in his biography, "Quality control was always foremost in our minds, because if a tool failed, it could kill someone, and since we were our own best customers, there was a good chance it would be *us*!"[9] Patagonia's sales took off when the firm began selling high-quality shirts that were more durable and colorful than anything on the market at the time. The firm's product offering shifted from climbing gear to outdoor clothing, but Chouinard's passion for quality remained steadfast. A colleague recalled how agitated Chouinard would become when Patagonia received product returns (for example, shirts with buttons that had fallen off). He demanded that his staff do whatever was needed to ensure that their products were of the highest quality—regardless of the effort or cost of doing so.[10] Chouinard sees his firm's two core values, protecting the environment and producing quality products, as closely linked. He wants

people to buy fewer products, but the products they buy must perform better, last longer, and, when possible, be recyclable.[11]

Some believe that corporations, when all is said and done, are
legal entities created to earn returns for their shareholders.[12] A
well-known business pundit argues this view when he says, "Here
is the truth: The DNA of a business is to maximize returns to its
shareholders."[13] Nothing more or less. Those with this view argue
that the concern that companies show for customers, employees,
and the environment may be sincere but are always secondary to
the need to maximize profits. The problem with this argument is
that many successful companies are dedicated to something beyond making money. Whole Foods says it wants to change the
world through better nutrition. Pixar strives to touch people
through its movies. Zappos sees its highest calling as creating happiness, not only for customers but for the world at large. Airbnb
wants to create a sense of belonging and community, providing
lodging where people feel at home wherever they travel. Those
with a cynical bent view these statements as public relations and
marketing ploys designed to enhance their brands. But these companies back up their lofty statements with their actions and investments. They fully understand the need to earn a profit—and the
consequences if they fail to do so. But they don't focus on profit as
their highest calling.

A small story from Zappos illustrates this point. Several years
ago the firm's founder and CEO was attending an all-day out-of-
town meeting with individuals from Sketchers, a manufacturer of
shoes. The group went back to the hotel after the meeting and too
many drinks at a local bar. They wanted to order a pizza, but room
service at the hotel was closed (as it was far past the 11 p.m. deadline). One person in the group suggested that they order out from a
pizzeria. Zappos CEO Tony Hsieh suggested, half in jest, that they
call the Zappos 800 number for ordering shoes. He said they should,
without telling the Zappos call-center employee who they were,
ask for help in finding a pizzeria that would deliver to the hotel.
Hsieh made a bet that the Zappos call-center employee would help

because his firm is dedicated to serving others—regardless of the request. One of the Sketchers people took the CEO up on his boast and made the call, with others in the group listening in on the speakerphone. The Zappos call-center employee was initially confused as to how to respond. But, as Hsieh predicted, she then helped locate the desired pizza. Tony Hsieh tells this story to illustrate that his firm's first priority is not selling shoes but, instead, creating happiness through service to others.[14] This statement is more than rhetoric at Zappos. The company, for example, trains team members on how to fully engage callers, with the goal of meeting their needs whenever possible. It wants each caller to Zappos to leave the interaction happier. The company does not use efficiency metrics (number of calls per hour) to reward its call-center employees. Nor does it promote "upselling," where callers are encouraged to buy more products beyond their initial purchase. Zappos likes to publicize that some customers stay on the line with its call-center reps for hours at a time (with a recent call breaking the firm's previous record in lasting 10 hours and 43 minutes). Paying its employees to stay on the phone for hours is hard to justify from a profit perspective—yet that is what Zappos does.

A paradox of cutting-edge firms is that they make more money because money is not what they care most about. In this regard, they don't act like the stereotype of a firm focused only on quarterly earnings. They are not even fixated on growth, even though many of them are among the fastest growing firms in history. Pixar, for instance, has produced a string of blockbuster films that in total have made billions of dollars. Pixar takes pride in its films being commercially successful and even rewards its employees with bonuses when a film does well. But revenue is not the firm's ultimate measure of success. Pixar's primary goal is to make films that touch people at an emotional level. This sounds idealistic, even a bit naive, but that's the goal. The Pixar film *Finding Nemo*, for example, was a commercial success in part because of its technical brilliance in animating underwater scenes. However, the film is a success because of a well-crafted storyline of an overprotective father learning to be a better parent. Other movie studios, or at least those seeking to maximize their financial results, would have quickly followed a hit like *Finding Nemo* with a sequel—and, in so doing, profitably captured the audience from the first film. Pixar, however, was not going to make a sequel just to cash in on an obvious commercial opportunity. It waited 13 years to make the follow-up film, *Finding Dory*, because the storyline wasn't yet up to its standards.[15] The cutting-edge firms in this book don't exist to make money, even though they are exceptionally successful. They make money because it allows them to do the work they love.[16] Profit, in these firms, is necessary and important—but insufficient as a reason for being.

Cutting-edge firms and their teams often have a religious, or more accurately a quasi-religious, quality to them. They are, of course, not aligned with any formal religion. But consider how they operate. First, there is shared belief in serving a larger purpose (better health, better planet, greater happiness). The goals vary across firms, but they are similar in their pursuit of something beyond making money. Second, there is a deep personal commitment on the part of their members to serve that purpose—which is not simply a slogan on the wall at the entrance of a company building or posted on a website under the banner "Our Values." These firms consist in large part of true believers. Work becomes more of a vocation than a job. Even when people could work fewer hours or take off during weekends and for vacations, many do not because work to them is much more than work. Third, these firms often believe they are special in regard to their purposes, capabilities, and histories. Each views itself as unique in its beliefs and practices—and, humility aside, superior to other firms. Each of these factors can create what some view as a religious-like culture within these companies—particularly to outsiders seeking to understand how they operate.

Most of these firms have origin stories showing how they came into existence and overcame obstacles to become what they are today. These are their signature narratives that bring to life the larger purpose of each company. In particular, they create a shared mindset about what is expected of people and teams within the company. The themes in these stories vary by company depending on its history and the values it wants to emphasize. But their intent is similar in communicating what each company wants from its people—how it wants them to think and act. Whole Foods, for example, tells a story about surviving the worst flood in 70 years in the city of Austin, where its first store was located. The store's inventory was ruined and most of its equipment damaged. The losses totaled over $400,000, and the recently founded company had no insurance. Customers and neighbors voluntarily joined the store's team members to clean up the damage so it could reopen. Creditors and vendors also provided help in giving Whole Foods time to recover and pay its debts. This story is on the company's website, and told to new hires, because it reinforces the passionate commitment of its employees as well as their connection to the local community—something that Whole Foods still values even though it is now a multi-billion-dollar corporation.

Going further, we can compare cutting-edge companies to cults. The comparison is inevitable given the degree of passion one finds within these companies, particularly when they are led by a highly charismatic leader who engenders a strong sense of loyalty. Zappos, for example, is very much the creation of its founder Tony Hsieh. His personality is stamped on most of the company's beliefs and practices. For example, he believes that the lines most people draw between their work and personal lives are artificial and unhealthy. He requires Zappos managers to actively socialize outside of work with others on their teams. Hsieh believes this fosters closer relationships and allows good ideas to surface more naturally. Managers who are unwilling to do so are not hired or don't remain with the firm. A second example of Zappos being an expression of Hsieh's thinking involves his dislike of hierarchy. He is now implementing a new organizational approach in Zappos with an emphasis on self-managing teams, called holacracy.[17] In the simplest terms, holacracy eliminates most of the authority structures found in traditional firms (including titles). This radical approach is designed to create a company of entrepreneurs who identify and seize opportunities as they arise and, in so doing, help the company operate more effectively. Traditional management roles are replaced by governance groups called "circles." These groups review and then approve or deny the improvement ideas generated by individuals. Members of the company then pull together as needed to execute an approved idea. The model is robust in having a set of formal group processes to surface, vet and act on new ideas, replacing the chain of command that is found in most firms. Hsieh believes holacracy will spark innovation in Zappos and allow it to thrive over the long-term.

As founder and CEO of the company, Hsieh is implementing his new organizational model even though some employees disagree with the approach.[18] Hsieh told them to embrace the paradigm or leave the company. Reports indicate that a significant number of his employees took him up on his offer, which included a generous severance buyout, and quit. Hsieh, of course, is not alone in being a leader who puts his imprint on the firm he leads. Patagonia largely embodies Yvon Chouinard's personality and values. The same is true for Whole Foods in regard to the imprint of John Mackey. The same for Reed Hastings at Netflix, Ed Catmull at Pixar, and Brian Chesky at Airbnb. These firms may not be cults, but they are very much the creation of their founders.

Comparing cutting-edge firms to cults, however, ultimately fails because the reality of running a business means that a leader's beliefs are always tested in the marketplace—they can't simply be based on the persuasiveness of those beliefs or willingness of others to join his or her cause. A business leader's ideas are proven over time to be productive or not. Tony Hsieh's willingness to try new approaches in pushing Zappos forward is admirable. But implementing holacracy is not simply getting people to believe what he believes. His organizational model will be tested against the results it produces in the marketplace with customers, as well as the impact it has on the firm's culture and people. Time will tell if Hsieh has pushed his company to the next level of its evolution or, in his zeal, has undermined what he and others spent years building.

A second reason that the cult analogy fails is that these cutting-edge firms work in ways that benefit not only their members but the world at large—unlike cults, often secretive, which ultimately take advantage of their members and are destructive to society. Airbnb, for example, is described by some as a cult-like company. Its founders shared an unwavering conviction that they could change the way people experience travel—facilitating room rentals among its hosts and guests. The firm's larger goal, however, is to foster trust and a great sense of community around the world—a lofty, ideological, almost religious goal. But the firm's business model, tested and refined, now produces millions of annual guest rentals in 91 countries.[19] It provides a benefit valued by millions of people. If Airbnb was a cult in the beginning, it evolved into something else—perhaps a contradiction of sorts in being a secular religion. The challenge for cutting-edge firms is to stay idealistic, pushing the boundaries of what it means to be a business without becoming detached from the need to attract customers and earn a profit. The challenge is to be cult-like without becoming a cult.

✦

In Chapter 1, I stated that extreme teams achieve two things above all else—deliver results and build relationships. More importantly, they push results and relationships to the extremes—far beyond what is found in more conventional firms. To this end, they need to attract individuals who are "all in"—fully committed and deeply passionate about their work and company. The term that best describes these people is *obsessive*, which is a state in which team members are constantly thinking about their work and company, and working diligently towards the achievement of their shared goals.[20]

I describe cutting-edge teams as obsessive because it suggests a level of commitment far beyond what is found in more conventional firms, where people may be professional but not completely immersed in their work. People who are concerned about work-life balance suggest that obsession with one's work is unhealthy both for individuals and their firms. This is often true, as evident in the Pixar "parking lot" story. But great success rarely happens without a critical number of people on a team or in a company who have this trait. Obsession may not be healthy, but it describes a core attribute of great companies and teams. The downside of obsessive behavior is the price to pay for doing something extraordinary.

Let's start with the obsessive nature of those who lead cutting-edge firms. Justine Musk is the former wife of Elon Musk, the highly respected founder of the car company Tesla and other ventures such as PayPal. She describes Elon's obsessive personality as a key to his extraordinary success:

> Extreme success is different from what I suppose you could just consider "success," . . . you don't have to be . . . Elon to be affluent and accomplished and maintain a great lifestyle. Your odds of happiness are better that way. But if you're extreme, you must be what you are, which means that happiness is more or less beside the point. These people tend to be freaks and misfits who were forced to experience the world in an unusually challenging way. They developed strategies to survive, and as they grow older they find ways to apply these strategies to other things, and create for themselves a distinct and powerful advantage. They don't think the way other people think. They see things from angles that unlock new ideas and insights. Other people consider them to be somewhat insane.[21]

Justine Musk's language is extreme in describing visionary leaders as freaks and misfits. But it is fair to say that these leaders are abnormal in their outsized drive to succeed and their complete immersion in their work. This is not to say that obsession, in itself, leads to success. There are plenty of obsessed people who lack the talent needed to be successful. The capabilities needed for obsession to produce "extreme success" vary depending on the demands on a leader and the specific challenges facing his or her group. In some situations, for example, a leader needs highly developed analytical capabilities. In other cases, the key is an ability to build partnerships and manage conflict across groups. But the inverse is equally true—there are highly talented people who lack the obsessive drive needed to produce something significant. These individuals may have more raw talent than others but lack the ability to realize their talent in contrast to those who are fixated on their work and are relentless in their desire to succeed.

There is much written about the so-called 10,000 hour rule.[22] It states that mastering an activity requires 10,000 hours of disciplined practice performing that activity. Talent is needed to obtain mastery, but mastery does not come without the necessary hours of deliberate practice. If we apply this rule to a sport such as tennis, this means that a highly talented athlete needs to practice every day for four hours for seven years. The player Andre Agassi said that he did more than that—he estimates he hit at least 2,500 balls a day from the time he was six years old. Close to a million balls a year. Ten million balls before he turned professional.[23] How many people, even those with extraordinary hand and eye coordination and in Andre's case unrelenting pressure from a demanding parent, have the resolve needed to hit that many balls? Imagine what is sacrificed in one's life to hit 2,500 balls a day, every day of your life. The same is true for the work done by visionary leaders in cutting-edge firms—they will stay with a task and strive to reach a goal to a degree that can only be described as abnormal.

Obsession, then, is essential to reach the highest levels of performance. But most people view obsession as a negative quality—a type of psychological disorder. In Japan, the word *karoshi* refers to those who die as a result of working around the clock. In English, it roughly translates into "worked to death and died like an ox." Japan, of course, is not alone in having a segment of its population that is addicted to work. In the United States, there is an association that calls itself Workaholics Anonymous. This group views compulsive working as a disorder, similar to other more well-known addictions such as drinking or gambling.[24] Work obsession, from this perspective, is an attempt to block out stresses in another part of one's life. There is always a risk that those with obsessive personalities become destructively consumed by their work, taking a toll on their health and family lives. There is a difference, however, between being obsessed and being addicted to work. Those who are obsessed, as I am defining the term, find meaning in their work and enjoy it. In contrast, workaholics do not—they use work as a means of avoiding something else in their lives that provokes anxiety or discomfort.

✇

Most think of obsession, even in its best form, as an individual trait—but it also describes cutting-edge teams. Examples include the team in Pixar that produced *Toy Story 2* and the Patagonia team that executed the firm's shift to organic cotton. A team's leader is often the catalyst for obsession, but a team will sometimes operate, at a collective level, in a likeminded manner. Most groundbreaking products, for instance, are developed by a small cadre of intense people who love what they are doing and the product they are creating. These teams often fade into the background, and the team leader becomes the focus of attention once a product is successfully launched. The Pixar team, for example, that produced the movie *Finding Nemo* is unknown to the public and even to a large degree within the industry. The film's director, Andrew Stanton, gets the accolades, which he clearly deserves, but it is his team that is ultimately responsible for creating that successful movie. This does not mean that a team consists of people with the same level of commitment or that a leader doesn't set the direction and tone for the group. But the group, and in particular its level of commitment to the task, is the key to success.

Obsession also works at a company level. Each of the seven firms profiled in this book have been described by outsiders and the media as being populated by true believers. They are portrayed as people who are consumed by their firm's mission and are "all in" in striving to make a contribution to its achievement. The founder of Alibaba, Jack Ma, touches on the role of obsession in describing how his firm operates. The following occurred after he gave a speech at Harvard about his company:

> After my talk, a CEO from a foreign company said that I was a mad man. He said he had been in China for many years, and didn't believe that my way of managing a company would work. I invited him to visit Alibaba. After a three-day stay, he said, "Now I understand. Here you have 100 mad men just like you." I agreed. People in a madhouse never admit they are crazy. They believe the outsiders are. That's why people here in Alibaba are united.[25]

Obsession comes in three, frequently interconnected, forms. The first, and most important, is an obsession with the work itself and resulting product. In many cutting-edge firms and teams, people view work as central to their identities—not something they do but something they are. Paul Graham, a well-known investor in startup firms, suggests that these people are ridiculously committed to what they produce—fixating, for example, on product details that customers don't even notice. These are also people who persevere and survive when others are defeated by the challenges they face.[26] Obsessive people work primarily to satisfy their own needs. Not the needs of customers or shareholders. Not the needs of those above in an organization's hierarchy. They strive to produce something they personally value that meets their own standards of excellence. In this respect, they are self-centered and even narcissistic in being their own customers. Their reasoning is that if they produce something they love, others will love it as well. Brad Bird, a respected director at Pixar, describes this philosophy as follows:

> If you say you're making a movie for "them," that automatically puts you on an unsteady footing. The implication is, you're making it for a group that you are not a member of—and there is something very insincere in that. . . . So my goal is to make a movie I want to see. If I do it sincerely enough and well enough—if I'm hard on myself and not completely off base, not completely different from the rest of humanity—other people will also get engaged and find the film entertaining.[27]

Even the emphasis at Zappos on creating happiness is not customer driven. It comes from the founder of the firm articulating a higher purpose for himself and, by extension, others in his company who hold the same belief. Customers benefit from that obsession, but they are not its source. It is also interesting to note that many of the cutting-edge firms are obsessed with a purpose that is distinct from what they sell. Patagonia says that it is not in the business of selling clothes. Zappos says that it is not in the business of selling shoes. Airbnb says that it is not in the business of renting rooms. These statements sound absurd because they appear to be denying how they make money—selling shirts, selling shoes, renting rooms. But these firms, and particularly their leaders, view these activities as secondary, or derivative, of that which truly matters to them. What they do, the actual work, is different than why they do it.

Another aspect of obsessing on work is a willingness to fixate over a long period of time on the task at hand. In particular, people and teams in these firms act with a relentless focus on getting it right. This is not to suggest that people in conventional firms and teams are not detail oriented or lacking in commitment; it is, however, to indicate that this behavior is more extreme in cutting-edge firms. People in these groups will obsess over details that others might gloss over or pursue only so far. Obsessed people and teams don't let go. People in Pixar, for example, view Walt Disney as an icon in the field of animation. In particular, they value his life-long dedication to his craft. His level of commitment to movie animation was evident in that he was still talking about the movie *Snow White and the Seven Dwarfs* decades after its completion. In particular, he was upset that some of the technical aspects of that film's animation were less than what he wanted because of the time and budgetary constraints his team faced when making the film. Snow White's facial features, in particular, weren't as consistently sharp as Disney wanted. He was concerned that "The bridge on her nose floats all over her face."[28] The film had long become a classic, but Disney was still thinking about what his team didn't get right 20 years earlier.

A second obsession of cutting-edge firms is an emotional investment in building a great company. As noted in the Chapter 1, cutting-edge firms deliver results and build relationships. A singular obsession with the work itself will often produce better results, at least in the near term. But an obsession with the work does not mean that relationships are valued. In fact, it can mean that relationships are seen as peripheral in comparison to the product or service being produced. Cutting-edge teams realize the risk in this approach and, instead, want people to be equally obsessed with the culture of their firms. They want those who are consumed not only with their work; they want people who are consumed with creating relationships that are the foundation of a great company. Again, consider Tony Hsieh of Zappos. The firm he founded prior to Zappos was an Internet advertising group. It was eventually bought by Microsoft for $265 million. Hsieh says he sold his first firm because, as it grew, he no longer wanted to work there. He notes,

> When it was starting out, when it was just 5 or 10 of us, it was like your typical dot-com. We were all really excited, working around the clock, sleeping under our desks, had no idea what

day of the week it was. But we didn't . . . pay attention to company culture. By the time we got to 100 people, even though we hired people with the right skill sets and experiences, I just dreaded getting out of bed in the morning and was hitting that snooze button over and over again.[29]

Hsieh wanted to work with people whom he enjoyed being around— which was no longer the case in the firm he founded. As a result, early on he focused on creating the culture he wanted at Zappos. The emphasis on creating an organization with the right environment surfaces in myriad managerial practices that make Zappos unique. For example, Zappos does not hire seasonal workers to help with the increased workload that comes with holiday sales. It believes that temporary workers will not necessarily possess the cultural values it wants and, as result, will compromise the larger culture if they are hired. Instead, people within the firm are asked to work longer hours to meet the seasonal demand. Zappos rejects a common industry practice, the hiring of seasonal workers, to protect the culture it values.

An obsessive focus on culture is found among all of the firms profiled in the book. The leaders of these firms spend much of their time working to get their cultures right. Each has a different view of what is the right culture—but each is clear on what he or she wants and doesn't want.A story about the importance of culture is found at Airbnb. That firm's CEO, in a note he sent to his employees, described a meeting he had just had with a major investor. The CEO and his team were reviewing Airbnb's growth plan, looking for support and guidance from the investor, who had deep experience working with a range of start-up companies:

Midway through the conversation, I asked him what was the single most important piece of advice he had for us. He replied, "Don't fuck up the culture." This wasn't what we were expecting from someone who just gave us $150M. I asked him to elaborate on this. He said one of the reasons he invested in us was our culture. But he had a somewhat cynical view that it was practically inevitable once a company gets to a certain size to "fuck it up."[30]

Airbnb's CEO took the investor's advice and initiated an internal review process in the company to identify what was important in the culture and what it needed to do to avoid its potential erosion. Alibaba is another example of a cutting-edge firm valuing its culture. The company is run by a unique partnership of 28 individuals—who collectively assume responsibility for the firm. Alibaba has policies that require future partners to have at least five years of tenure with the company and a strong record of promoting its unique mission, vision, and values. No one can become a partner unless he or she is an advocate for the culture and committed to sustaining its core attributes.[31] Jack Ma maintains that outsiders, those he calls *airborne troops*, should never be allowed to hold the most senior positions within a company, including CEO—as they can't understand the firm's culture and its importance to the firm's survival.

N

A third obsession of cutting-edge firms is the desire to have an impact on society—in most cases, this involves improving the world through one's products, services, and way of operating.[32] The CEO of Whole Foods tells, for example, how early in the firm's history some wanted his company to focus only on its most dedicated consumers and, in so doing, sell a limited set of products (no sugar, no meat, no processed foods). He rejected this recommendation because he wanted his company to have a broader impact in society. He writes, "Whole Foods is not a business for a clique, or for the elite . . . . We wanted to change the world."[33] "That is what animates me personally. That is what animates the company." Other highly visible firms have a similar view of their missions.[34] The new leader of Apple's retail stores, Angela Ahrendts, spent most of her first six months on the job visiting 40 different markets, interacting with new colleagues. She concluded afterwards that the company was successful primarily because of its strong culture—one dedicated to changing people's lives and leaving the world better as a result of its efforts. These are lofty words, but in her mind, they describe the essence of the company she just joined. The strength of Apple's culture surprised her despite everything she read about the company—a culture that she didn't fully appreciate until she joined it.[35]

Academic research underscores the importance of working with a purpose. Amy Wrzesniewski, who teaches at the Yale School of Management, examined how people view meaning in their work.[36] She found that the majority of people view their jobs as a way to earn money. They are employees doing their jobs. But some people, up to one-third of those she studied, felt their work was connected to a higher purpose. This purpose typically took the form of helping customers or benefiting society. She found that people who view their work as a calling are more satisfied with their jobs, work longer hours, and take fewer days off. Other research suggests that people whose managers emphasize the higher meaning of their work are more dedicated to their firms and less likely to leave their companies for other jobs.[37] In short, they view their companies as more than businesses and their work as more than jobs.

The leaders of the firms profiled in this book all meet the three obsessive criteria noted here. They have an unrelenting focus on their work and the products they make. They love their companies and see the cultures they have created as their crowning achievements. They strive to have an impact on society—wanting to "make a dent in the universe."[38] These obsessive qualities are each important in their own right but are most effective when pursued in combination. In particular, leaders and teams who obsess only on their work without an equally strong commitment to their companies and society run the risk of becoming toxically self-absorbed. In contrast, embracing the work, company, and society turns obsession into a positive quality.

Yvon Chouinard, for example, cares about the environment and the quality of his products. He is not particularly charismatic as a leader but is unwavering in his beliefs and willingness to act on them. If he focused only on the quality of his products, Patagonia would be a good but not a great company.

$$\mathcal{N}$$

Obsession is closely related to what some call grit—the "passionate commitment to a single mission and an unswerving dedication to achieve that mission."[39] Grit is what obsession, at least its productive form, looks like in action. The research on grit began with an effort to understand why some individuals are successful and others fail. Angela Duckworth, the University of Pennsylvania professor who did the pioneering work in this area, studied people in a variety of settings—including the military, schools, and companies. She found that the most important predictor of success, beyond intelligence and social awareness, was grit.[40] The research found that high achievers are successful, in part, because they are better able to overcome the inevitable obstacles and challenges that arise in the pursuit of their particular passions.[41] An important point to note, however, is that grit is not simply tenacity—it also requires a commitment by the individual to a higher goal. This is the case because success is not just the ability to persevere when others give up—it is moving deliberately toward a goal to which the individual is passionately committed. In particular, the findings indicate that people with grit are better able to persevere when facing the inevitable setbacks that occur in any great undertaking.

The research on grit focuses on the thinking and behavior of individuals. But grit within a team may be even more important in that most endeavors involve some element of collaboration. Any complex and challenging initiative almost always requires a team, or team of teams, to achieve the desired result. Team members, in the best case, push each other in ways that increase commitment to a shared goal and sustain motivation to achieve that goal. A real-world example of grit is the ability of Airbnb to overcome problems early in its history when it encountered a security issue in one rental unit. A property in San Francisco was ransacked by an Airbnb renter, and the personal property stolen. The host posted a detailed description of what happened online, including her disappointment in how Airbnb's staff worked with her after the event. Her post then went viral—creating media headlines and concerns on the part of some homeowners who were allowing strangers into their homes. Airbnb was largely unprepared to deal with the crisis, as well as the larger problem of security and safety. The firm, at the time, had a customer-support hotline that consisted of an answering machine that was checked once a day. It failed to hire the staff needed to manage this type of problem and had no formal protocol in place to deal with a crisis. The firm's response, as a result, was slow and ineffectual in meeting the needs of the host whose home was damaged. Brian Chesky, CEO of Airbnb, described the event as "a crash course in crisis management . . . . We felt paralyzed and over the last four weeks, we have really screwed things up."[42] He said, "We should have responded faster, communicated more sensitively and taken more decisive action to make sure she felt safe and secure. . . . But we weren't prepared for the crisis and we dropped the ball. Now we're dealing with the consequences."[43] Airbnb, after its initial missteps, pulled together a team to develop and implement a variety of measures to address the problem, including the doubling of its security staff (a group that now has over 600 people) and offering what eventually became a $1 million host guarantee program (which pays for damage resulting from a rental). Airbnb also developed, over several years, practices to give both its hosts and guests more background information about each other, in order to increase the level of comfort felt by each. The firm's safety processes continue to evolve and now include verifying the identification of those renting rooms and user ratings of both hosts and guests. Airbnb, demonstrating its grittiness, used the initial crisis it faced to improve how it minimizes risk of future adverse events and, in so doing, increased the level of trust among its users.

N

Obsessive teams have greater upsides and downsides than conventional teams. The dilemma is that you don't get the upside without risking the downside. These teams can, for instance, obsess on the wrong things, as the obsessed are always fixated on something. Just because a group is obsessed doesn't mean that it is obsessed with the right thing. Many teams, for example, fixate on near-term results and, specifically, delivering on their quarterly financial targets. In itself, this is not a bad thing. But they do this in some situations to the point of undermining the actions and investments needed to sustain long-term growth. Obsessed teams can also strive, in their passion, to do something that can't be done—and in so doing waste a great deal of time and money. They ignore useful data and feedback and stubbornly push forward in an inflexible manner. They refuse to kill projects that should be killed earlier rather than later. Moreover, obsessive teams can be perfectionistic and fail to understand the tradeoffs that exist in any business or product—resulting in missed deadlines and blown budgets. They are more likely to burn out their own team members with unreasonable demands and excessive work hours. Obsessive teams can be so task focused, so lacking in empathy, that they damage relationships within the teams as well as with those in other teams. Their members are narrowly focused on achieving their objectives and often lack the emotional and political skills needed when working within a company. These groups can also go rogue, seeing those above them in a firm's hierarchy as being hostile to what they want to achieve and, in so doing, alienating those whose support they need. All of the above are potential problems once obsession enters the picture—all with very real downsides. This is the reason that many firms don't want people and teams that are obsessive. But far worse is a group where people are simply doing their jobs—even if they do them well. Obsession is the foundation for making great things happen. Beige doesn't win in business.

➡ *TAKEAWAYS*

> ➤ Cutting-edge firms have a critical mass of obsessive people and teams.

> ➤ They view their work as a calling—much more than a job to be done.The team members align around a higher purpose that shapes their collective thinking and behavior.

> ➤ Their obsessive nature is both a blessing and a curse— necessary to achieve something extraordinary but potentially destructive if not managed well.

3

VALUE FIT OVER CAPABILITIES

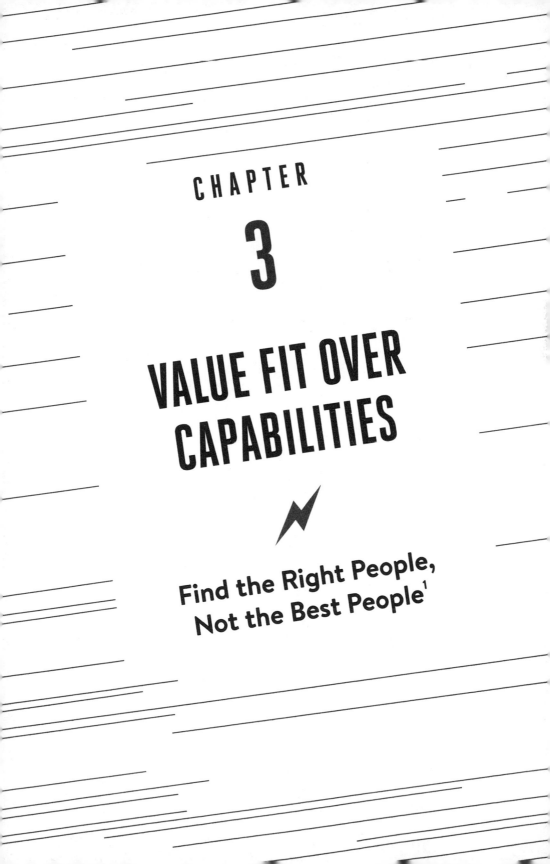

Find the Right People, Not the Best People[1]

Zappos is in the enviable position of having more than 100 job applicants for every position it fills.[2] Hiring the right person, however, can take months if not years at the e-commerce apparel firm. Its new screening process begins with people joining an online community called *Zappos Insiders*. Those who sign up are assigned "company ambassadors" to help determine if they should pursue a job with the company.[3] These employees interact digitally with potential applicants, answering questions about the firm and its culture. The ambassadors also meet, when helpful, with people in restaurants, bars, and company social events near its Las Vegas headquarters. The next stage is a formal interview with the hiring manager and members of his or her team. The goal of these meetings is to assess a candidate's capabilities in relation to an open job. Those who pass this test then have another interview, conducted by the firm's human resources staff, to determine if they fit the unique culture of Zappos. These interviews are not done by the hiring manager because Zappos is leery of the "halo effect," which occurs when a candidate's technical capabilities are so strong that similar strengths are assumed in other, nonrelated, areas (such as one's values). The decision to hire someone is based 50 percent on a candidate's capabilities and 50 percent on his or her fit to the culture. The company refuses to hire those who have great resumes if they don't value what the firm values. They do this even knowing that taking time to find the right people, rejecting those who are highly capable but a poor cultural fit, doesn't pay off in the near term—that having open positions takes a toll in meeting the firm's near-term performance targets.[4] They value their culture more than achieving their quarterly targets.

Zappos uses specific questions to assess each applicant's fit to its culture. At least one interview question is asked for each of the firm's 10 values.[5] One set of questions, for example, focuses on the ability of potential hires to "wow" others through their service to them. Zappos is built on a belief in extraordinary customer service and wants to ensure that new hires bring that orientation with them. Questions in this area include "What's the best work-related compliment you've ever received?" and "What's something that you did at work that maybe no one else knew about but you are very proud of?" A different set of questions probes if a potential hire can "create fun and a little weirdness" (another core value of the firm). Applicants are asked to rate how weird they are on a scale from 1 to 10 and then describe something they recently did that was weird. Zappos believes that work should be fun and that weird people are simply more fun to be around. Not many companies would assess a candidate's weirdness, but Zappos is serious about the need for a fun work environment. Zappos also uses other data to assess candidates. For instance, it observes how candidates interact with people when they make their initial visits to its company building. Those who act in ways that contradict the firm's values are rejected. There are cases where highly qualified applicants were rejected because they were rude to the company shuttle bus driver who picked them up at the airport on their arrival.

Those who make it through the hiring gauntlet at Zappos are then required to complete a rigorous four-week training program, much of which focuses on understanding and living the firm's values. The training also includes a stint taking customer orders in the firm's call center. The firm's new-hire training is required for its most senior as well as its most junior people—there are no exceptions. In one case, the firm took a year and a half to locate the right person to fill a senior role. The firm then fired the individual just weeks after his arrival. He made the mistake of believing that an orientation program was optional. He was terminated after arriving late for two sessions. He indicated, on his way out, that he didn't understand the firm's seriousness in regard to its cultural values.[6] After the training, the company then makes what it calls *The Offer*. Each new hire is asked if he or she wants to quit the firm and be paid to do so. The company only wants to keep those who are "all in." The Offer has increased over time and now equals $2,000.[7] Zappos indicates that only 2 percent of its new hires take the offer, but the impact on the 98 percent who remain is significant in affirming their commitment to the company. They walk away from a payout to stay with the firm.

The stronger and more unique the culture of a firm or team, the more important fit becomes.[8] This is one reason that firms such as Zappos and Patagonia initially hired only friends of the founders. Cutting-edge firms are passionate about their beliefs and have particular ways of operating—and, as a result, they can be less welcoming of those who don't share their world view. Patagonia, for example, looks to hire people who are actively involved in sports such as climbing and surfing (so-called *dirt bags*). People who prefer to sit indoors and watch TV, or those who don't care about the environment, will feel out of place at Patagonia. The firm's founder notes, "This is a unique culture, extremely unique. Not everyone fits here. I've found that rather than bring in businessmen and teach them to be dirt bags, it's easier to teach dirt bags to do business."[9] Patagonia believes technical and professional skills can be taught—but a passion for the outdoors is innate and thus part of the firm's selection criteria. Cutting-edge firms would rather hire, if forced to do so, people who are "A's" in regard to cultural fit and "B's" in regard to their talent.[10]

✦

A leader's job, in large part, is hiring and motivating the right people for a particular task. The ability to assess the capabilities of individuals and then determine how they will work together to produce a desired outcome is more of an art than a science. That said, I find in my consulting work that the skill of assessing talent varies widely among leaders. Some leaders are simply much better than others at assessing people's current capabilities and their future growth potential. Leaders also vary in their ability to assess how people will work together, how they will gel, when working together within a team. Think of any great endeavor and the critical element of staffing it with talented individuals who can collectively deliver what is needed. If a leader fails at this task, efforts to make a group or team more effective "downstream" are likely to fall short. The lesson from cutting-edge firms and teams is that cultural fit must be a key factor in making their hiring decisions. Leaders also need to create formal and informal practices that increase the likelihood that managers at all levels will do the same in making their hiring decisions.

Arguing that cultural fit is essential raises the question of how to define *culture*. The simplest definition is that culture is "the way things are done around here." Each firm has particular patterns of thinking and behavior, which develop over time as a firm overcomes challenges in its efforts to survive and grow. However, as the scholar Ed Schein notes, these patterns of behavior are more complicated than the routines within a company. They derive from deeper-level assumptions, particularly in regard to what is needed for the group to be successful. Netflix, for example, is a culture that believes in the primacy of talent—that is, the firm believes that the company or team with the best talent will produce the best results and win in the marketplace. This may appear self-evident, but other firms, with different cultures, hold different assumptions. For example, some believe that the company with the most robust processes or the best technology will deliver the best results.

There are several risks when resumes become more important than cultural fit. The first is that those who don't fully buy into a firm's mission and way of operating are in most cases less likely to give their all to make their company or team successful. As a result, the upside of having individuals and teams who are "all in" is lost or at least diminished. This need is a challenge, in particular, as a firm grows and hires hundreds if not thousands of employees. They need to have people on hand to manage the growth, to meet near-term demands, and thus the screening filters can become less disciplined. There is also more demand on a firm's leader's time as a result of growth, and vetting candidates can easily become less important.

A second, more extreme, risk is that those who don't fit a firm's culture become toxic to that culture. Most of the attention goes to hiring those who are embodiments of a firm's culture, but in some cases, the impact of those who are at odds with a culture have a greater impact.[11] For example, Zappos strives to create an optimistic work environment where people believe in the company's goal of increasing the level of happiness in the world. Those who are cynical, perhaps believing that happiness is an inappropriate or unrealistic goal for a business, can influence others through what academics call emotional contagion. This possibility is supported by research that indicates how a toxic employee can have a negative impact by infecting others with their attitudes as well as their behaviors.[12] A final risk is that people who don't fit a firm's culture are more likely to hire others who also don't fit the culture. They are also more likely to tolerate behaviors in others, once hired, that are at odds with the firm's cultural values and norms. Hiring the wrong person, then, is more than making a bad decision about one individual—hiring a bad fit puts the larger culture at risk.

A final risk is that those at odds with a firm's culture will not be able to get things done within that culture. New hires sometimes fail because they either don't understand how their new culture works or understand it but devalue it. This does not mean that a newcomer needs to blindly follow what others expect or blindly accept the status quo. It does, however, mean that an awareness of a group's culture is essential to working effectively within that culture. A highly visible case of cultural failure occurred at Nike years ago when it appointed an outsider to be its new CEO. William Perez had worked in his previous firm for more than 20 years and came into his new job with an impressive set of skills. He lasted, however, only 18 months with Nike, in part because adjusting to its strong culture was too great a leap. Those who reported to him never rallied behind him, and he remained an outsider in their eyes despite being the CEO of the company.[13] The same challenges hold true for new hires at all levels within a firm. Cultural fit is a key to influencing others and getting them to work with you in a collaborative manner. Even those brought into a company or team as "change agents" are often on the losing end of the culture dynamic—they fail because they don't understand how to operate within the culture they are striving to change.

Cultural fit is particularly important when staffing initial positions within a company or team. The tone set by early members of a group impacts subsequent hires and, as a result, has a disproportionate influence on the group's emerging culture. Therefore, great care is needed in selecting a group's first hires, ensuring that these individuals fully embody what leaders want to see in their groups. Brian Chesky, the founder and CEO of Airbnb, took a great deal of time to hire his firm's first employee. He spent five months reviewing thousands of resumes and conducting hundreds of interviews before making an offer to the engineer. He explained why he took so much care in making that hiring decision:

> Some people ask why did you spend so much time on hiring your first engineer. I think bringing in your first engineer is like bringing in a DNA chip to the company . . . if we're successful, there were going to be a thousand people just like him or her in that company . . . . There was something much more long-term and much more enduring which was, do I want to work with one hundred thousand more people like this?[14]

Chesky didn't do this for just the first employee. He hired the first 300 employees of the firm—screening the applicants and conducting the interviews. He was looking for those he described as missionaries—people who believed in the firm's mission. One question he asked to identify this trait was, "If you had just ten years to live,

would you take this job?" The importance of hiring those who believe in Airbnb and its higher purpose is expressed in the comment
of one employee regarding the firm's culture:

> Airbnb really doesn't hire people unless they are passionate
> about the product, its implications and its future. You can be
> off the charts in terms of brains, experience and technical
> skills, but if you come off as blasé about what we do, you won't
> get hired. I think that really distinguishes us from other com-
> panies and ensures that we're all invested in the company's fu-
> ture, not just financially.[15]

The former human resources leader of Netflix noted how her firm,
as well, placed great emphasis on hiring "true believers" in the for-
mative stages of the company: "Here's what you want in your first
100 employees: the best talent you can afford, who work hard and
believe . . . The belief part can actually outdo the other two. It's
more than passion . . . . People need to believe."[16]

⚡

There are potential downsides of being too focused on hiring those
who are a cultural fit. A team that values cultural fit over experience or capabilities may fail to hire or promote necessary talent.
The result is a company of people who work well together, people
who collectively share a set of values, but don't collectively have
the skill needed for their company or team to win in the marketplace. Most firms, cutting-edge groups included, look for a threshold level of capability before cultural fit is considered in the hiring
or promotional process. The question, however, is, what does a
group do when it needs someone who is far above threshold in
talent—perhaps even world class in a particular area that is critical
to a firm's success (such as finance or logistics)? The easy answer is
to hire people who are both world class and a good cultural fit. In
reality, such people are difficult to find. The question then becomes,
what level of compromise is acceptable in regard to talent or cul-

ture? Cutting-edge firms, as noted, are less likely to compromise on the cultural side, in contrast to more conventional firms, which are more likely to compromise on the cultural side. These firms may not even view cultural fit as a factor in making their hiring decisions, or they may rationalize a candidate's poor cultural fit because the capabilities of that individual are so impressive.

Another risk in valuing fit over experience is that a firm or team can become monolithic in hiring only those who fit a particular style. Culture fit, if not determined skillfully, can screen out people who don't fit a narrow definition of what each firm views as a model employee. All things being equal, differences among team members in a group or team enhance the ability to manage complex challenges.[17] The way cutting-edge firms deal with the risk of being too homogenous is to ensure that their people are first committed to the firm's purpose and core set of values. Then they embrace differences in background, thinking, and style. Pixar is particularly notable for its willingness to take risks on people who are different than others within the company. In particular, it goes out of its way to bring in people who don't know the "Pixar Way." The goal is to deliberately hire those who will challenge the status quo within the firm and, as a result, make the firm stronger. The director Andrew Stanton, for example, had not touched a computer when he was hired to direct the computer-animated film *Finding Nemo*. Stanton, however, believed in the core values of Pixar—with the most important being the centrality of great storytelling and the need to develop a cohesive team. With those core beliefs, he could bring into the company new ideas and recommendations.

An emphasis on culture also requires removing those who, once hired, turn out to be a bad fit. Pixar, for example, hires highly talented and creative people—but they must have an ability to work in a team environment. This doesn't mean that people are any less intense or less open in expressing their points of view. In fact, Pixar wants strong-willed people who will challenge the status quo. Teamwork, however, requires that they work well with others, in their own team and with those in other teams, in the very complicated and challenging process of making an animated film. The firm's CEO noted:

> [At Pixar] there is very high tolerance for eccentricity, very creative, and to the point where some [of our people] are strange . . . but there are a small number of people who are socially dysfunctional [and] very creative—we get rid of them. If we don't have a healthy group then it isn't going to work. There is this illusion that this person is creative and has all this stuff, well the fact is there are literally thousands of ideas involved in putting something like this together.[18]

/

The first task in hiring for fit, hiring the right person, is determining what you stand for as a company or team. Most large firms have a set of values that define their ideal cultures. Go to their websites and you will see their values listed. All good. All nicely worded. These values, however, often fall short on several fronts. The first is that many firms develop a set of values that are so general that they have no real impact on people or their behavior within a firm. You find, for instance, many companies that value integrity and teamwork. But what company or leader doesn't want integrity and teamwork? For values to be meaningful, they need to fit the specific mission of a company and have an idiosyncratic bent to them. There needs to be some authentic edge to the values that are essential in realizing the firm's purpose and values. The notion of "dirt bags," for instance, uniquely fits the history and mission of Patagonia. It's that firm's fingerprint—no other company strives to hire and retain dirt bags.

A second mistake is to develop a long list of values that cover everything that could possibly be important to a company or group.[19] The result is a set of values that people either don't remember or don't use to guide their behavior (as there are simply too many to follow). The problem is that people have difficulty internalizing many values and, more importantly, choosing between these values when conflicts arise. For example, a firm suggests that delivering results is an imperative but so is delighting customers. These two values are often synergistic, but there are cases where they conflict (for example, when meeting a customer's request will cost so much that it hurts the group's ability to deliver profit). Which has priority? Organizations that hire talented people expect them to make the right call in this situation. However, too much ambiguity causes problems because different people and teams will focus on one value more than the other. A researcher at the University of Pennsylvania, Andrew Carton, studied this problem in hospital settings.[20] He found that the performance of a hospital improved if the leadership articulated a clear vision for his or her organization. The key variable, however, was having fewer organizational values (no more than four) and then ranking those values from most to least important. In so doing, the leaders gave people the context they needed to make decisions when conflict among values arose.

Another, related, problem occurs when a group's values are often defined at such a high level that people don't know what they look like in action. Values should be defined in terms of expected behavior—defined in both positive terms (you should do this) and negative terms (you should not do this). Teamwork is a common value—but what does it mean in a particular firm at a behavioral level? Pixar, for example, tells its people that anyone in any group can talk to anyone in another group if he or she has a question or idea. No need to go up the hierarchy for approval to do so. In this case, teamwork means communicating across group boundaries in an open and direct manner ("talk to anyone you like without permission to do so"). Each company, and in some cases each team, needs to define its "vital few" values in specific behavioral terms that give people a clear sense of what is expected of them.

A third mistake in regard to values is the failure to link them to a firm's objectives and work practices. For example, a firm may indicate that it values customer service above all else but it has no objectives linked to customer service and no way to measure the customer service it provides. Or it fails to link its hiring, promotion, and reward practices to the value it places on customer service. In these cases, the firm's values are aspirational, with no follow through to make them come alive within a company. Each of the cutting-edge firms in this book has carefully determined how to link its values to the rewards it offers its employees and, in the negative, the consequences if people violate those values. In this respect, cutting-edge firms are more likely to reward and punish based on how people perform in regard to their values. It is not only a matter of people and teams delivering results—how those results are delivered is just as important.

A final mistake, and perhaps the most damaging, is for a company to articulate its values and then work in a manner that violates them. That is, they espouse one set of cultural beliefs but act on a different set of beliefs. They may, for example, say that talent is all important but then invest little time or money in attracting or developing talent.[21] A well-known example of a conflict between espoused versus actual values is the energy company Enron. The company, no longer in existence, had a set of values that included integrity. It claimed to work with customers openly and honestly. It then acted in a manner that set the benchmark for unethical behavior in defrauding its customers. Less extreme but more common are firms that promote people who behave in ways that are at odds with the values they embrace. For instance, a firm talks about the importance of results and then promotes someone who repeatedly fails to deliver on his or her performance targets. Or a firm says that it values teamwork and then promotes someone who has delivered results but in a manner that is anything other than collaborative (hoarding information from other groups, failing to share resources, or undermining colleagues who are viewed as competitors, for example).

N

Valuing fit over experience in the hiring and promoting of people requires a clear awareness of the single most important quality needed in those who work for a company. A range of cultural values may be important, but one should take priority. For example, Patagonia has gone through various cycles during its history in hiring people. It started by bringing into the firm friends of the founder—people who were like him in their beliefs and lifestyle. As the company grew, it increasingly looked for people with more traditional business backgrounds and specialized skills (what the founder calls the MBA types). After a number of these people failed in their roles, the firm went back to its roots. It looked for people who were closer to its original hires in being outdoor types with a commitment to environmental causes. As noted in the last Chapter, the commitment to the firm's central beliefs should be deeply felt—an obsession. Those who work for Whole Foods need to love natural food. Those who work for Pixar need to love storytelling. Those who work for Zappos must love serving others. A major benefit of being a purpose-driven firm or group is that you know what you are looking for in new hires and attract like-minded people. Whole Foods, for example, looks for people who are committed to improving others' well-being through food. The firm has a clear identity, and this allows it to attract those who value what it values. The firm's CEO notes,

> Increasingly, the talent is finding its way to us. We don't tend to lose people, and in my conversations with Team Members, when I ask, Why did you come to Whole Foods? They say, I did my research, and I want to be in a company that has values. I want to be part of something larger than myself.[22]

In this respect, the cutting-edge firms and teams are looking for people who are pursuing something beyond paychecks or the advancement of their careers. They are missionaries who believe in the cause to which the company is dedicated.

There are two additional traits that are important to ensure a good cultural fit. As noted in Chapter 1, cutting-edge teams want people who push the extremes on both results and relationships. Each company has its own way of operationalizing results and relationships, but the goal is the same. Pixar, for example, looks for an ability to deliver results by asking potential hires to describe one thing at which they excelled in the past. It can be work related or more personal (such as a hobby or sport far removed from Pixar's business). The goal is to find individuals who have reached a high level of excellence in an area of interest to them—believing that those who have done so, who know what excellence feels like, will also do so in their work at Pixar. The firm wants those who have experienced excellence and know what it takes to achieve mastery in any given area. At Airbnb, the founders pursue a similar line of thinking in asking potential hires to describe something they have done in their past that is exceptional. That firm's CEO notes that in his interview process he looks for people who are dreamers that make things happen. He says,

> I also ask people to summarize their life in three minutes. I'm trying to figure out the formative decisions and experiences that influenced who you are as a person. Once I figure that out, I'm trying to understand the two or three most remarkable things you've ever done in your life. Because if you've never done anything remarkable in your life until this point, you probably never will.[23]

There are many ways to screen for those who can build relationships. Greg Brenneman, chairman of CCMP Capital, uses what some call the airplane test. He asks himself after interviewing a candidate,

> If I were to get on an airplane with this guy or gal, would I want to fly across the Atlantic with them? Are they nice people to be with? Do you want to be with them? Because I find that people that don't relate well to anybody, from owners or board members to peers to direct reports to folks that actually work for a

living in the trenches, they don't succeed very well. You can usually tell that by asking, "What do you enjoy doing? What do you do as a hobby?" And ask a few questions to the people that work around them, and you get a pretty good sense pretty quickly.[24]

A different version of this interview screen is the "copy machine" test. In this case, you ask yourself if a potential hire is someone you wouldn't want to see in the hallway if you happen to be working late in the night. You are tired and don't have time to deal with someone who is difficult to interact with—someone you don't really want to see when you are trying to complete a difficult task.[25]

Other firms, such as Zappos, take a more direct approach in assessing a candidate's ability to build relationships. They ask potential hires, "Do you feel you are a better individual contributor or a better team player? Which do you prefer?" "When was a time you 'took one for the team' even though it wasn't your responsibility?"[26] Other firms may pose questions about past successes, screening for self-glorifying responses. They may look, in particular, for applicants who describe accomplishments in terms of a group's achievements (versus a more self-centered achievement). When someone's description of his or her greatest accomplishment starts with "I did this" or "My results were . . . ," it can be a red flag—a sign that the person is overly self-centered. Other firms probe the person's ability to build lasting relationships. Alan, founder and chief executive of the technology firm Pegasystems, is a leader who understands the importance of relationships in organizational performance. He takes the following approach in assessing the relationship capabilities of a potential hire:

One question I've found to be extremely powerful as a predictor of how well people will do in customer-facing roles is to ask for specific names of people they've worked with as those people moved between companies or roles . . . . And I'm really quite specific, and I ask them if it would be O.K. to talk to those folks. A lot of people don't have those sorts of relationships. I find that to be a really useful predictor of whether they are relationship-oriented, which I think is important not just for dealing with customers—it's important for dealing with people inside the firm as well.[27]

The key is to find those who can partner with others to produce what is needed and, more generally, help build a sense of community with the company or team. One of my clients, for instance, believes that self-awareness is essential if people are to work well together. He asks each interviewee to summarize the conversation that he had with them in the interview. More specifically, he says to the interviewee at the end of the meeting, "I am going home tonight and will tell my wife about my interview with you today. What do you think I will say to her?" His goal is to assess how well the person is reading his or her impact on others versus seeing only what he or she wants to see. The assumption in asking this question is that a more self-aware person, one who "reads" the interview and interviewee accurately, will have greater success in building relationships with others in the firm.

Cutting-edge firms and teams, then, look for fit on three attributes in making their hiring decisions:

1. Belief in the Firm's Higher Purpose: Is the person "all in" in his or her support of the firm's core purpose? Does he or she have the necessary passion if not obsession regarding the firm's reason for being?

2. Ability to Deliver Results: Does the person have the drive, temperament, and skill needed to deliver necessary results at the highest level?

3. Ability to Build Relationships: Does the person have the drive and temperament needed to develop close working relation-

ships with his or her team members and with those in other teams?

Each firm or team needs to determine how to screen applicants for each of these three attributes, which will vary depending on the firm and how it defines success in each area. An additional complication is that the process is not simply identifying individuals with these necessary skills and traits. It also requires an assessment of how each individual's traits will mesh with others in a specific team—that is, how people in a group will interact to produce a desired outcome. The level of teamwork required, of course, varies with each task, but most complex endeavors involve working with others to achieve a desired outcome. Hiring people, then, is not just hiring them into a position as individuals. It is hiring them into a team with a number of other people with a diverse set of capabilities, values, and styles. Those making a hiring decision need to assess how well the various members of a team will work together

Viewing cultural fit in this manner means that team members must complement each other, must develop the right chemistry, if the value of the team is to be fully realized. This doesn't mean, however, that members are clones of each other. For example, the degree of focus on results and relationships needs to be the right mix within a team to produce optimal outcomes. In particular, a group that is heavily results oriented will benefit from having some members who are more relationship focused. Inversely, a group that is heavily relationship based will benefit from adding those who are more task focused. In this way, the group is more likely to have a necessary level of both attributes. Members, including a team leader, who bring a different focus in regard to results and relationships bring something that may be lacking–versus simply reinforcing or replicating what already exists within the team.[28] This benefit, however, is undermined if the person doesn't value or have threshold skills in both results and relationships. In that case, the person will most likely be rejected by the team because he or she doesn't possess the basic cultural traits needed to be successful in that particular group and firm.

 **TAKEAWAYS**

> ➤ Most firms hire based on a job candidate's resume—assessing how well his or her skills fit the demands of a specific job.

> ➤ Cutting-edge firms, in contrast, place equal if not greater emphasis on a person's fit to their culture.

> ➤ Cultural fit is important in three areas: each person must embrace the group's higher purpose, the value it places on results, and the value it places on relationships.

> ➤ The best firms and teams develop robust processes to screen for these traits in the hiring and promotion of their people.

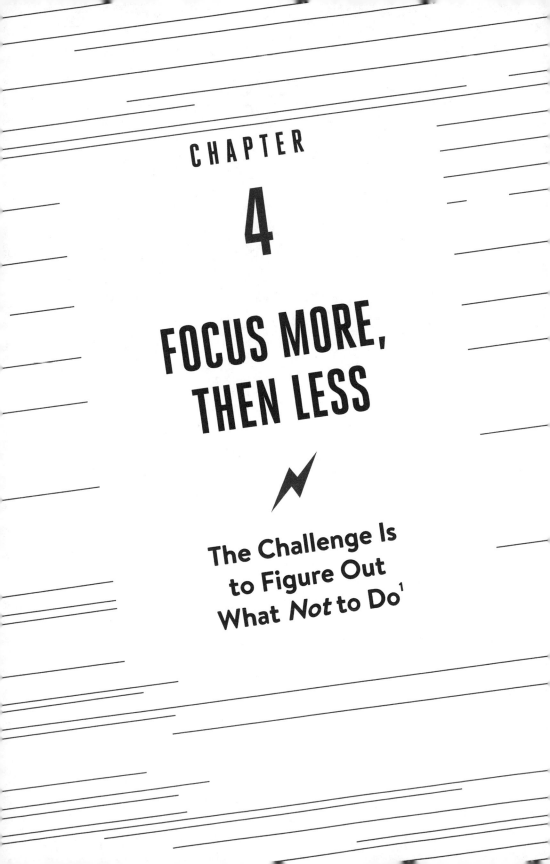

CHAPTER

4

FOCUS MORE, THEN LESS

The Challenge Is
to Figure Out
What *Not* to Do[1]

Airbnb is the world's largest peer-to-peer lodging company. It has more rooms for rent each night than Marriott and Hilton combined, quite an achievement for a company that began less than a decade ago.[2] In 2016, the company hosted its 100th million guest.[3] But there were no elaborate plans when the company booked its first rental—just two young men offering a room in their apartment to those attending a business conference in San Francisco. The founders were primarily interested in making their rent through additional income. However, in meeting their own needs, they were playing with a big idea. Millions of rooms in houses and apartments were going unused. They wanted to help people rent these rooms, using the Internet as a tool to simplify and enhance the process. But their idea was based on an audacious proposition—that people would invite strangers to stay in their homes. The founders created a website to profile the rental listings, with the goal of making renting a room in another person's home no more difficult, and no more risky, than booking a room at the Marriott. The new company was called Airbed & Breakfast after the air mattresses placed on the floor of that first rental.

In the early years, the founders positioned the company as offering less-expensive and more-personal lodging than the hotel chains. Its singular focus, like many startups, was unambiguous—survival. Objectives, if they existed at all, covered what needed to be done in the next two weeks.[4] After a few years, and the hiring of hundreds of employees, the firm's leaders devel-

oped an annual company operating plan with a dozen key objectives. This plan eliminated some of the confusion that inevitably
comes with a rapidly growing company. But it also created a new
problem—notably, it was difficult to sustain focus and allocate resources within the company across so many priorities. Airbnb, for
example, was partnering with vacation-rental firms that served
as brokers who provided rooms to travelers. Airbnb was also
building a loyal following of customers who were renting rooms
directly for their own personal use. Vacation firms offered an opportunity for Airbnb to expand quickly, but the individual traveler
was still its core customer. Both groups were important, but more
effort was going into developing products and services for the
rental firms (given the near-term benefit of doing so). The downside was that less was being invested in the development of products for the firm's individual users due to the limits of the
engineering resources within the company. Recognizing its mistake, Airbnb clarified the priorities and redeployed its resources.
The lesson learned, however, was that more is not better when it
comes to priorities.

The following year, Airbnb streamlined its objectives. It settled
on four goals and a few success measures.[5] All four goals were
summarized on a single sheet of paper—with the goal of advanc-
ing those initiatives that would have the greatest impact on the
long-term growth of the firm. *The Sheet*, as it came to be called
within Airbnb, listed each of the four objectives, its target completion date, and an internal owner. Simplifying the firm's priorities and getting them onto a single sheet, was difficult. It took a
team of people within the company five months to determine the
priorities. Having 10 priorities is easier, at least initially, than having 4 priorities in that it doesn't require hard choices. But pursuing 10 priorities is close to having no priorities. Every firm and
team has limits in regard to staff, time, and resources—and thus
needs to focus on the areas that have the highest return on investment in relation to its growth strategy. The other factor that
makes prioritization difficult is the risk inherent in doing so.

Covering all the bases, placing many bets, spreads a group's risk—or at least the appearance of risk. Focusing only on a few priorities means that those few priorities had better be the right priorities. Focus also requires that those selected priorities be executed at a high level. Otherwise, failure to do so will be evident to all. Airbnb, for instance, has recently focused on developing its mobile toolkit—viewing it as essential to drive its growth and meet its customers' needs. Success in its mobile platform is easy to monitor, at least at a basic level in terms of users. Failure to achieve its targets in this area will be evident both within the firm and to its investors.

◢

Airbnb learned, through its own experience, the importance of focusing on a small set of vital few priorities. It did this initially because it had limited resources and needed to focus on that which it could afford in terms of time and resources. The problem it faces now is the opposite. It has ample resources and can afford to pursue any number of good ideas. The concern, at this point in its growth, is that it becomes less focused and less willing to invest in its core business, which is enhancing the experience of its guests and hosts. One of the firm's CEOs describes this as the "tyranny of choice"—a problem that comes when a company has plenty of resources and is highly empowering of its people and teams.[6] This "high-class" problem can be as challenging as not having enough choices. Airbnb has also learned the importance of cascading its priorities in an effective manner. A great deal of effort in Airbnb goes into communicating the key priorities to its employees, including the reason each is important and how success will be measured. The intent is to make sure that people at all levels understand what is critical to the firm's success. Then, and this is key, each person and team at Airbnb is responsible for figuring out how to best support the company-wide priorities. In essence, the firm is saying to its people, "Here is what we want to achieve and why. You need to determine how you and your team can add the most value as we pursue these goals." This approach ensures a broad understanding of what the firm must do but also keeps ownership for specific tactics and decisions at the lowest possible level.

At a broader level, Airbnb wants its people to determine how to best support the brand on which the firm is built—which centers on the idea of belonging. The company strives to provide its guests and hosts with a highly personal experience of being part of a larger community.[7] It believes the people want an experience of community and connection, in contrast to staying in a more impersonal hotel. Toward this end, Airbnb broke down the experience of travelers into 15 discrete steps, starting with a guest finding a room on its website, followed by successive steps in a trip, including what it calls the moment of truth (when a guest first walks into rental), being "out and about" in the community, and providing feedback at the end of one's stay. Airbnb leadership continually asks its people and teams how their work, both ongoing and proposed, helps provide the best possible Airbnb experience in one or more of these key steps. People at Airbnb thus understand their firm's overall value proposition (creating experiences that enhance a sense of belonging for a traveler) and, within this context, its annual set of three or four company-wide priorities. Managers, teams, and employees must then determine the areas in which they can add the most value and how to work in a manner that best achieves those objectives.

The role of managers at Airbnb, unlike most companies, is not to set goals for their team members or tell them how to operate.[8] Engineers at Airbnb, for instance, are engaged in the goal setting and planning of all major projects. They determine what needs to be done and how to measure success. The company then goes one step further—it gives its people the freedom to select which projects they want to work on.[9] Airbnb engineers are encouraged to change teams if there is another project within the company that better matches their interests or skills.[10] This practice is based on the belief that people do their best work and have the greatest impact when they are involved in projects that are of personal interest to them. This approach makes sense when one realizes that Airbnb values, above all, experience—and, more specifically, enriching the experience of its customers as well as employees.[11] Top-down control, from this viewpoint, is not a way to enrich experience or, more generally, build community. Airbnb doesn't tell its hosts what to charge for a room or how to decorate their lodgings. It also gives them the option of not renting a room to guests who have lower ratings on the firm's feedback forms. In a similar manner, Airbnb believes in giving employees a great deal of say in the workplace. It doesn't tell them how to prioritize their work or how to go about achieving their objectives. It doesn't even tell them where they need to work, as people can move about the corporate office and select an area that works best for them. Leadership will, however, ask how the work of a particular team or individual supports the firm's overall mission and, in so doing, ensures that their efforts add value. The company also wants accountability for results once a goal is decided on. But that is a very different process than dictating the "what" and "how" of people's work.[12] Once there is alignment at each level with the company's overall objectives, the role of the manager is to help his or her team members obtain necessary resources and overcome obstacles that would hinder their progress.

N

Getting everyone to align around a set of priorities begins with context setting. The goal is to ensure that everyone understands the environment in which a company operates, as well as the strategies it will use to be successful in that environment. *Context*, a term that Netflix coined in regard to its culture, explains the "why" of a firm's specific priorities, including the opportunities and threats facing it. This requires clarity on the part of a group's senior management on the business environment in which they operate. At the minimum, people within a company need to understand the following:

→ Why do we exist as a company—what is our reason for being?

→ How do we make money? What drives our results?

→ Who are our most important customers?

→ What products or services do our customers value the most?

→ Who are our competitors—existing and emerging? What threats do they pose?

→ How do we measure our success as a company?

→ What is our plan to win in the marketplace?

→ What capabilities do we need to be successful?

→ What values are most important to us?

→ What behaviors are expected of us as members of the company?[13]

Even in a senior team, where we would expect people to be highly aligned, there is often a lack of agreement on the above questions. One study, for example, found that more than 90 percent of CEOs believe that their team members both support and actively communicate their firm's strategic priorities. In fact, only 2 percent of their leadership team members, when asked, listed the same top three strategic priorities for their companies.[14] Another study asked people to rank the most significant challenges in building global teams. Two of the top five challenges noted were obtaining clarity on the team's objectives and aligning the goals of its individual members.[15] The need, then, is be clear about the context in which the firm or group is operating—and then build alignment starting with one's own team. One test of how well a group's context is communicated is to ask people within the organization to delineate their firm's key objectives and strategies. The answers people give to this question are often wrong, incomplete, or inconsistent.

Netflix, in particular, believes that context setting is necessary to sustain what it deems essential to its success—namely, a freedom and responsibility culture. The company maintains that the best outcomes occur when the context is effectively communicated by a firm's leaders and managers. When done well, context allows people to make informed decisions about their priorities and even their day-to-day work. When managers do not provide context, those who report to them are more likely to do foolish things (such as invest time and money in areas where it doesn't make any sense). Setting the right context, however, is not dictating the outcomes of decisions or what employees need to do. Instead, it provides the information and understanding that others need to make informed decisions. This is not to suggest that the line between setting context and ensuring alignment on Netflix's objectives is always clean or easy. In some cases, senior leadership may be more involved in the details that some at the lower levels might prefer. But Netflix believes that setting the context is the opposite of the top-down approach found in many traditional firms— an approach that Netflix believes undermines employee initiative and slows down decision-making as people wait for higher-level managers to determine the best course of action. A top-down approach can also demoralize people, particularly the "creative types," who want more autonomy in determining the actions they need to take in any given situation. Managers at Netflix are expected to clearly communicate what the firm is striving to achieve and what success looks like in terms of expected outcomes, providing as much detail as needed in regard to quality, time parameters, and cost. The employee then determines, within these parameters, what is needed to achieve success.

N

Creating the right context supports how Netflix wants to operate in what it calls a highly aligned but loosely coupled organization. The company insists that people be in agreement about the environment in which they operate and their overall goals but have the freedom to do what is needed for them and the company to be successful.[16] Netflix describes this as follows:

Highly Aligned means . . .

→ Strategy and goals are clear, specific, and broadly understood

→ Team interactions are focused on strategy and goals, rather than tactics

→ Large investment in management time required to be transparent, articulate, and perceptive

Loosely Coupled means . . .

→ Minimal cross-functional meetings except to get aligned on goals and strategy

→ Trust between groups on tactics without previewing/approving each one—so groups can move fast

→ Leaders reaching out proactively for ad-hoc coordination and perspective as appropriate—occasional post-mortems on tactics necessary to increase alignment[17]

The emphasis on setting context in Netflix was born of a near-death experience. In its early years, the company spent a great deal of money on the expectation of rapid growth. But sales failed to materialize at the pace that leadership anticipated, and startup financing became much harder to obtain. As a result, layoffs occurred, along with a newfound emphasis on cash flow management. One insider noted,

> We were spending huge amounts buying DVDs, setting up distribution centers, and ordering original programming, all before we'd collected a cent from our new subscribers. Our

employees needed to learn that even though revenue was growing, managing expenses really mattered . . . we had a meeting every week in the parking lot. We called it the metrics meeting, and we'd hand out a piece of paper with nine charts showing exactly how much money we had in the bank, how many customers we had, you know like a basic P&L.[18]

Setting context, of course, is not a one-time event in response to a financial crisis or the rollout of a new strategic initiative. A group's business environment inevitably changes, and ongoing communication is needed to ensure that people's understanding evolves in sync with those changes. Many leaders, however, mistakenly assume that team members understand what has changed in the firm's environment and the resulting impact on priorities and behaviors. They assume, in short, that others have the same understanding as themselves in regard to that changing context. Other leaders are at fault for lacking the patience needed to engage others in understanding the broader environment in which they now operate.[19] They don't see this as important and consequently fail to invest the time needed to set the context.

Once a group has a shared context, it needs to identify the few business priorities that will drive it forward. In some cases, firms have a clear set of priorities but become distracted by less important concerns that they then strive to address at a high level of effectiveness. This is what some call the "good plow, wrong field" phenomena.[20] For instance, a firm may focus on improving its operational efficiency, which, all things being equal, is a good thing. But all things are rarely equal. In this case, the firm's success requires that it develop exciting products that win new customers and grow revenue. This is not to suggest that operational efficiency is unimportant—only that efforts to improve efficiency are less critical than growing revenue in this particular company. Work that goes into targeted areas needs to be assessed relative to other initiatives, perhaps more important initiatives, that also require resources and attention. Projects and issues outside of these areas are distractions that don't offer the same return to the business.

Setting priorities also requires agreement on what "falls off the plate." This sounds obvious, but many groups are reluctant to say what activities or projects will be minimized or stopped. Instead, they assume that it can all be done or done all at once (versus sequencing what needs to be done to ensure necessary resources and focus). The result is that people have more than they can accomplish and end up selecting on their own what they believe is the most important. The other outcomes is that people simply try to achieve more than can be done and suffer the consequences. The ability to focus requires saying no to some initiatives. Netflix, for example, decided early on that it would not compete with Blockbuster at a "brick and mortar" retail level. The firm's founders assumed, correctly, that the Internet would be the demise of retail stores in its industry. Patagonia is an even more extreme example in deciding that it didn't want to grow too fast, as expansive growth posed problems for a firm with its values and culture. The CEO noted, "You have to know your strengths and limitations and live within your means . . . . The sooner a company tries to be what it is not, the sooner it tries to 'have it all,' the sooner it will die."[21]

Distractions for teams come in a variety of forms. In some cases, these are lower-value priorities that a team strives to achieve. Distractions also come in the form of administrative tasks that take time away from the crucial work that needs to be done. For instance, some firms want team leaders to submit a monthly report of progress against their objectives. These reports, if not done well, are a time-consuming "check the box" exercise that doesn't promote productive dialogue or action. Another time drain comes in the form of too many meetings across a company. For example, people are pulled into higher-level reviews and meetings that take time better spent with their own teams and customers. This is not to say that meetings are always unnecessary or unproductive—but many meetings consume more time than needed, with a resulting opportunity cost to those involved (that is, they take time away from more important pursuits). A third type of distraction is political. In this case, competing factions and other forms of dysfunctional behavior within a company pull people into political battles that consume their energy with little return. One role of a team leader is to protect his or her team from unnecessary distractions that divert the group from the vital few priorities on which it must focus to be successful.

✳

There is no shortage of opportunities and challenges facing leaders and their teams. They can easily generate a long list of necessary initiatives. Some leaders believe that pushing people to achieve more results in higher levels of overall performance. That is, giving people 10 things to do is better even if they accomplish only 8 things (compared with giving them 5 things to do, all 5 of which they achieve). The problem with this logic is that the achievement of the truly critical areas may be undermined because people simply can't focus on them or the resources needed are not properly allocated. A related mistake is to have priorities that are overly complex. A test of simplicity is to ask people how they would explain to a family member the priorities being pursued within their company or team. These family members don't know the details of how the group operates, but they need to understand the priorities. If you can't explain them in a way that they understand, your priorities are too complex. Others use a test called the *elevator speech*. This requires that you place yourself in an elevator with someone and explain a single priority to him or her in the time it takes for the elevator to go from the first floor to the top floor of the building. This doesn't mean that a firm's priorities or challenges are simple or that a simple explanation is always better. It does mean, however, that the priorities need be explained in simple and memorable terms if they are to be internalized by the organization's members and have the desired impact.

There are several guidelines in developing a clear set of aligned priorities. The first is to have a very simple and easily explained set of goals (which are often updated annually but can be longer or shorter in duration depending on the situation). The most common mistake that groups make is having too many priorities, which was the case early on at Airbnb. The company now has a clear description of each company objective, along with a target date and internal owner. The goal, according to the firm's CEO, is to focus on fewer but higher-impact goals and include just enough detail that people know when the company has achieved, or not, the desired outcome. A second guideline in creating clear priorities is spelling out the desired outcome in clear and, if possible, measurable terms. These are the "success metrics" that delineate how progress will be measured for each priority over time. For example, a firm or team may have a specific revenue target for the first year after launching a new product. This is an example of an "outcome" measure that delineates the desired result. In contrast, a process measure describes an activity or task but not the end result. A process measure might be to "launch a new product incorporating the lessons learned regarding forecasting from our previous product launches." In most cases, groups want to develop a few outcome measures versus process measures because these measures don't dictate the "how" but do specify the "what." Ensuring that everyone agrees on their shared goals is more important, initially, than how those goals will be achieved.[22]

The best way to develop success measures varies across teams. In general, it is often helpful for team members to be involved in crafting the measures that they will use to assess their own progress. Involving people in the development of metrics helps ensure that the metrics are linked to the broader context and that everyone buys into them as goals they value. The risk is that a team, in the spirit of being inclusive and complete, embraces either the wrong measures or too many measures. Each team leader, and group, needs to cut back the measures it uses to prevent the performance scorecard from growing too large. In some cases, however, the degree of autonomy teams have in developing success metrics is more limited due to the nature of the work or a company's culture. Whole Foods, as noted earlier, has a group of metrics that it requires of its in-store teams (such as monthly sales and profit per employee). Each Whole Foods team is required to use these metrics to assess its performance. Whole Foods then links each team's performance on these metrics to rewards that are paid monthly. In this case, the measures are mandated, but the way the teams go about achieving their goals is not.

An additional benefit of having a clear set of "vital few" priorities is that it creates a bond among those working to achieve a shared goal. Groups within an organization can easily become isolated and operate in silos with conflicting goals.[23] The typical approach is to cascade the objectives and associated scorecard from the top down, with each level explaining its goals and measures to the group below.[24] I have also seen cases where peer teams that are dependent on each other will share their goals to ensure necessary understanding and alignment. A research and development group, for example, will meet with the manufacturing group within its company to ensure necessary coordination on moving products from R&D into production. Some firms go even further and make the goals of each team transparent. In this case, the priorities and success metrics of each group, at each level, are posted for everyone to see. Those groups that are even more aggressive also post the results of each group for others to see.

A third important area to consider in regard to priorities is accountability. Each team needs to decide if the group in total is responsible for each priority or, instead, if there is a point person or subgroup that takes the lead. These "owners" then work with the larger team as needed to deliver on the specified target. Assigning owners for priorities doesn't absolve the group from its collective responsibility, but it does clarify who is the go-to person or subgroup in moving a particular priority forward. Many leaders, as is the case in Airbnb, feel that having a single point of accountability results in greater progress (versus everybody owning everything). Netflix calls these individuals decision owners. The other important area to clarify, once accountabilities are assigned, is the authority that owners have in pushing a priority forward. For example, can these individuals and teams spend a project's budget without the approval of others above them or in other groups? Can they determine a product's specific features or cost? The intent in clarifying authorities is not to be overly rigid but, instead, to avoid the confusion that comes when authorities are unclear or in conflict.[25]

A fourth guideline in priority setting is developing effective ways to review a group's progress over time in each area. Some groups develop clear priorities but don't have a robust process to check their progress over time. In the worst case, priorities are developed, communicated, and never reviewed again (or reviewed only at the end of the year in a manner that does not allow for midcourse corrections). Cutting-edge teams, in contrast, have weekly, monthly, or quarterly reviews where progress is assessed using specific numeric targets or a more general system of assessment. One element of creating a robust review process is to encourage transparency at a peer level in regard to performance—versus simply having team members reporting out to their supervisor. Some teams, for example, develop a scorecard with color codes to assess progress (such as red, yellow, or green indicators to signal progress in each area). These review meetings, however, should not be a rigid reporting out of scores on a set of metrics. Instead, cutting-edge teams create an environment where performance is actively discussed and go-forward actions debated. The greatest benefit in having a scorecard is promoting a productive and timely discussion among team members (in contrast to a process that is designed to simply identify those who are underperforming). Peer visibility and feedback around a set of priorities or even work product is a powerful means to focus and motivate people to higher levels of performance. For this to occur, there needs to be clear metrics and a high level of trust within a group to allow for a candid discussion about progress and the causes of any gaps in the team's performance.

N

Cutting-edge firms and teams relentlessly focus on executing a small set of key priorities. In so doing, they avoid being distracted—pulled into peripheral activities that take time, energy, and resources away from what is truly needed to achieve something extraordinary. This means saying no to some proposals that show promise. It also means making tough choices to ensure focus. Netflix, for example, moved from DVDs to streaming online as quickly as possible—knowing that streaming was the key to its future success. The transition took longer than the firm anticipated, but the shift in its revenue was dramatic once the change took hold in the marketplace. Reed Hastings was adamant that the company avoid the fate of Kodak, a once-dominant firm that clung to its existing business model too long and missed the digital revolution in photography. He wanted his leadership team to eat, sleep, and breathe streaming. But the company retained its DVD business, which became an increasingly smaller, but highly profitable, segment of its revenue.[26] At one point, the company had 30 vice presidents, 5 of whom were dedicated to its DVD business. Reed decided that the DVD vice presidents should no longer attend the leadership meetings—as the firm needed to focus in these sessions only on streaming. This was not an easy decision, given the history of the firm and close-knit nature of the team, but Hastings believes it was the right decision to ensure necessary focus.

An apparent contradiction that characterizes cutting-edge firms and teams is that they also experiment with new ideas both in regard to their core business and outside of their core business. Getting that balance right is difficult, but they realize that too much focus, if not balanced with experimentation, can result in a business that fails to adapt to new opportunities and threats. As a result, they continually enhance their core business while also being managers of newness.[27] The goal is to try something that has not been done before and learn from the experience. Airbnb, for example, was founded on the belief that people would respond to an online rental site that was more detailed and engaging than other sites that existed at the time (such as Craigslist). The founders, on putting up their website, focused on providing high-quality photographs of their rental properties (as it reduced guest anxiety about staying in a unit they had never seen). They stumbled on the importance of photographs when staying with a host who had a great apartment but poor-quality photographs in her rental listing. This occurred before smartphones made taking photographs easier, and the owner of the unit was not savvy on uploading files from her camera to the firm's website. The founders asked her how she would feel if someone would come to her apartment to take the photographs for her—that she could push a button and a photographer would appear free of charge to shoot her apartment. She said that it would be magical. The next morning, one of the founders came back with his camera and took the photos. Airbnb slowly expanded this option for hosts and now has thousands of freelance photographers around the world taking professional-quality shots of their hosts' rental units. Airbnb looks for incremental improvements in its guest experience by using what it calls a *seven-star design* process.[28] Its guests provide ratings on a five-point scale at the end of each stay. The firm almost always gets the highest rating, but believes there is still opportunity to improve (in essence, it found that many people are easy graders). It asks its various teams, each focused on different parts of the traveler's journey, what would need to happen for guests to give their visit six stars (if that was an option on the grading scale). They want people to contact Airbnb and say that they want to add a star to the rating scale because they were so pleased with their experience. Why? Perhaps the host knew their favorite food or what they like to read and provided those when they checked into their room. Then the Airbnb team is asked what would be needed to get a seven-, eight-, or even nine-star rating. Many of the ideas generated in this process are outlandish ("Banners with guests' names on them are paraded through the airport when they arrive"), but the intent is clear. Think outside the box and make the experience of the traveler more memorable.

Each of the firms in this book can tell similar stories about how they improved their core business. Netflix, for example, has algorithms to determine what people like to watch and how they watch it (for example, sporadically or binge). They can then suggest titles that fit each customer's personal preferences and viewing habits. These successes, however, hide the fact that most experiments fail. Airbnb's first three website launches failed to attract customers, and it was only the fourth launch that proved successful. But cutting-edge firms keep pushing for new approaches, testing them often at a small scale and then taking those that appear promising to the next level of execution. The challenge is to keep one's company or team resolutely focused on its key imperatives while also testing new and innovative ideas that will drive the firm's future growth. This happens in areas both great and small. The CEO of Airbnb, for example, wants people to consider what a competitor might do to undermine or even kill his firm's business model.[29] That is, he wants his people to actively envision products or services that would render Airbnb's business model obsolete. The goal is to ensure that Airbnb innovates faster than the competition and, in so doing, prevents others from doing what Airbnb is now doing to traditional hotels with its peer-to-peer model. Airbnb is constantly testing new ideas within its current model, such as hosts picking up their guests at the airport or providing them with walking tours and other experiences (for example, dinners or cultural events). It has also considered other areas in the "sharing economy" outside of its current business. The problem, of course, is that firms invest in a particular operating model and, especially if successful, are slow to recognize when that model is at risk. Being rigidly focused on a narrow set of priorities, if not balanced with an ability to consider creative alternatives, can hurt a company over the long term.

Pixar also sees the risk when firms and teams replicate their current practices and, in so doing, risk becoming stagnant. In particular, Pixar doesn't want to simply repeat what worked in one film in another film. The CEO of the company, Ed Catmull, believes Pixar should deliberately strive to avoid what worked in the past and, instead, try something new. In terms of movies, this means not going back to an old storyline or even the emotions evoked in past films.[30] One way to encourage experimentation is to bring outsiders into a company or team. As noted in Chapter 3, there is a core set of beliefs and values that are needed for someone to become a team member. But a company like Pixar will deliberately hire outsiders in order to bring new perspectives and ideas on how to make the firm and its films better. This is the case even though Pixar is one of the most successful movie studios in history. It hires people, particularly directors, with very different backgrounds in terms of their training and experiences. The goal is not simply to get team members to think outside the box but to include people who come into the group thinking differently (because of who they are and what they have experienced). The ideal is to embrace people who are natural dissenters but can operate within the existing culture of the firm—pointing out opportunities as well as blind spots in how the company is operating. The goal for Pixar is to avoid becoming a clone of itself—which is easy to do in its industry, where sequels are often highly profitable but break no new ground.

One way to encourage innovation within a larger enterprise is to use teams to experiment with different models and approaches as they go about their work. These groups, in other words, are encouraged to incrementally innovate within their firm's current business model to improve its performance. Whole Foods decided early in its history that each of its stores, and even more importantly, each of the teams within its stores, needed to have a great deal of autonomy in determining the products and services that fulfilled the needs of its local customers. The decentralized design of the company was also thought to encourage innovation as each team experimented with new practices. One store in California, for example, decided to open a wine and craft beer bar inside the store. Whole Foods had sold wine in many of its stores for years but no store in the company had a wine bar. The California store, located in Sonoma County, came up with the idea, which is not surprising given its proximity to some of the finest vineyards in the world. Within months, the Whole Foods bar was generating more income than many of the other departments within the store, including seafood. The bar, however, was not simply a new profit center. It was part of an ongoing effort in that store to create a sense of community with its shoppers. Other stores took notice and studied what was done in the California store, assessing whether they should also have a bar. Whole Foods now has more than 75 bars in its stores across the country.[31]

Consider another example of local innovation in Whole Foods. Two team members saw an opportunity to offer health and well-being services to other businesses (a business-to-business model different from anything Whole Foods had done in the past). The company liked their proposal and supported their experiment. The resulting program, called Full Spoon, helps employees in participating companies improve their health. They get a 20 percent discount when they buy foods at Whole Foods that are marked as healthy. They also can participate in programs that track their diet and exercise habits and attend educational seminars designed to improve their health. The Full Spoon program is only offered today in a few stores but will most likely expand to other regions of the company if successful.

Incremental innovation is also found at Netflix, which believes in giving its teams a great deal of autonomy to come up with new ideas and, more importantly, the responsibility to make them work. A few years ago, a team within Netflix realized that some of its customers wanted to watch a complete set of shows in rapid succession. A sign that people liked to binge watch was evident from those ordering DVDs that contained an entire season of a particular TV show and then watching the episodes in rapid succession. The company knew that a customer might watch a full season or two of Mad Men in one weekend. As Netflix moved into providing on-demand streaming of shows over the Internet, it realized that many people wanted to do the same—which Netflix viewed as being similar to reading multiple chapters of a book at once. The innovation occurred when developing the show *House of Cards*. Netflix decided that all 13 episodes of that show's first season would be released at the same time (versus the historical practice of releasing one show per week over an entire TV season). This relatively simple but bold idea came about because the members of one Netflix team thought that a simultaneous offering of an entire season was simply giving customers what they wanted (which was to watch the show they wanted, when they wanted it). The company, based on a monthly subscription model, did not need to cater to advertisers who were paying for prime-time spots, which could be assured only with a traditional approach of one show per week (what some call "appointment TV"). *House of Cards* was a hit and accelerated a revolution in the industry in supporting the binge watching of shows. A recent survey indicates that more than 90 percent of TV viewers now engage in binge watching, which it defines as viewing more than three episodes of a show in one day at some point over the course of a year.[32]

Cutting-edge firms also productively defocus by encouraging people and teams to innovate outside of their core businesses. A well-known case is Google. Engineers in the firm are encouraged to spend 20 percent of their work time on personal projects unrelated to their current responsibilities—taking time to play with ideas of interest to them and see if they can develop a new product or line of business for the company. The founders of the company noted over a decade ago, "We encourage our employees, in addition to their regular projects, to spend 20% of their time working on what they think will most benefit Google . . . . This empowers them to be more creative and innovative. Many of our significant advances have happened in this manner."[33] This approach is not without problems because the company doesn't require or monitor the allocation of employees' time (who, in this case, are mostly engineers). Those who want to spend the 20 percent do it on their own with the company's blessing. However, many don't have time in their current demanding jobs to dedicate to outside interests. When Marissa Mayer left Google to become the CEO of Yahoo, she noted, "It's funny, people have been asking me since I got here, 'When is Yahoo going to have 20% time? . . . I've got to tell you the dirty little secret of Google's 20% time. It's really 120% time."[34]

The leaders of Google understand the challenge of finding time to innovate beyond one's current project. But they believe the 20 percent rule is best deployed without formal guidelines or mandates. The value of experimenting is what they want to instill within their culture—notably, the value of playing with new ideas that will generate new business opportunities.[35] Another approach to fostering productive defocusing is found at Airbnb. Each week, the firm has what it calls "demo days." People in the company demonstrate for others, usually those from other teams, what they are working on. This allows for people to get out of their own areas of responsibility and learn from those doing very different work. This supports the development of people as well as the potential areas of innovation across groups.

A related practice in cutting-edge groups is to encourage experimentation through fast failures. The concept is that work products, both in existing projects as well as out-of-the-box innovations, should be surfaced and tested on an ongoing basis. This stands in contrast to individuals or teams that spend long periods of time on a piece of work, seeking to refine it, before getting feedback from their peers or customers. The power of fast failures is evident in the film company Pixar. It conducts fast-cycle reviews in what it calls dailies. These are meetings where a team reviews the work in progress of animators to promote feedback, both positive and negative. During the hour of each morning's dailies, the group will review the shots of selected animators. The company wants work that is far enough along to be critiqued but not so far that it is set in stone.[36] In that meeting, the director of the film, other animators, as well as anyone else who wants to join in looks at the shots and discusses changes that would improve the work. A secondary benefit of the process is that animators whose work is not being reviewed learn from the feedback given to their peers. The logic of the dailies is that people waste a great deal of time, and limit their own creativity, when they strive to perfect something before showing it to others. Failure is viewed as a given in any creative effort, and Pixar wants those failures to be addressed faster—which allows for necessary changes earlier in the work process. This requires that people be comfortable showing work that is incomplete and getting feedback on it (which, of course, can be painful because work in progress is often not very good). Pixar strives to create a culture where people are comfortable, or at least less uncomfortable, reviewing their work with peers and obtaining direct but supportive feedback to see if they are on the right track.

 **TAKEAWAYS**

> ➤ Cutting-edge firms actively communicate the broader context to their members (market opportunities and threats, financial realities . . .).

> ➤ They then clarify their vital few strategic priorities—the three or four goals that must be achieved to move the firm or team forward.

> ➤ These priorities are defined in a manner that ensures that everyone knows what success looks like, including performance metrics and accountabilities.

> ➤ Cutting-edge firms, however, also understand that too much focus can be self-defeating—thus, they foster ongoing experimentation in an attempt to identify innovative customer and revenue opportunities.

CHAPTER 5

PUSH HARDER, PUSH SOFTER

Every Great Culture Embraces a Great Contradiction

Most firms operate with either a hard or soft edge.[1] Those with a hard edge emphasize the need for clear performance targets, disciplined practices, and absolute accountability for results. These groups are typically more formal and process driven. Think General Electric. Firms with a soft edge emphasize the importance of strong bonds among people working in a highly creative, sometimes chaotic environment. They are more informal and talent driven. Think Google. No firm or team is entirely hard or soft, but most favor one over the other based on the demands of their business, their individual histories, and even the idiosyncrasies of their leaders. This preference becomes, over time, part of a firm's DNA—replicating and shaping the way people think, feel, and behave. The challenge is to create a work environment that embraces what is often a messy contradiction—a work environment that is at once both hard and soft. Cutting-edge firms, and their teams, do just that.[2]

The simplest definition of *culture* is "the way we do things around here." Each company, and to some extent team, develops its own way of operating—distinctive in a manner similar to the way that personality is unique to each individual. Culture includes the core beliefs and assumptions that people have about their work, their company, and their competitive environment.[3] These deeper-level elements of culture function at both a cognitive and emotional level. Cognitive beliefs center on what people think, particularly in regard to the factors that will result in success or failure within a team or company. For example, Pixar employees believe that a great story with memorable characters is the key to making a film that people love. Story takes priority over everything else. Other studios may believe otherwise—perhaps thinking that savvy marketing or technical innovation drives a film's success. We can debate the degree to which each studio's beliefs are true (or more helpful), but people at Pixar are convinced that great films are the result of great stories. This is an example of a core assumption that influences how people behave within the company.

Cultures, at their core, are more than just assumptions that people share—they evoke feelings and emotions.[4] This element of culture, while related to assumptions, is more basic and visceral. The emotional connection that people at Pixar have with their films—and even the emotions they have about particular characters in those films, such as Woody in *Toy Story* 2 or Dory in *Finding Nemo*—goes beyond the need to tell a good story. We can imagine other film studios where people believe in the power of a good story but are far less emotional about their work. They may, for example, operate in an analytical manner with a focus on what storylines will appeal to a target audience. While Pixar is certainly savvy in marketing its films, that knowledge is not what drives people within the company. People's emotions, and even their personal experiences, are critically important in the making of its films. People at Pixar want their stories to move people, but the story needs to move them first. Pixar has one of the most disciplined processes in its industry for making animated films, processes that are incredibly complex and highly disciplined—but it never forgets that emotion is at the core of its business. Most of those who write about culture emphasize its cognitive elements—what people believe and the assumptions they hold about their firm and the world around them. But culture, more importantly, is based on emotions that arise from people's experiences working in a company and, more specifically, in a team. Culture, from this viewpoint, is more about emotions than beliefs and assumptions. Culture can be viewed as "how we do things around here" or "what we think around here." But more important is "what we feel around here."

An emphasis on experience, and the emotions that arise from experiences, originated in some cutting-edge companies with a focus on customer experiences. Starbucks, for example, stated that its goal was to be the "third place" for people to go after home and work. For that to happen, customers needed to feel comfortable in its stores and feel that they were part of the community (just as many people in the United Kingdom feel connected to their local pubs). The firm's CEO, Howard Schultz, emphasized that Starbucks was about the experience of being in its stores. That experience, particularly the interaction of its baristas with customers in the making of a coffee drink, was at the core of its brand. Schultz wrote in his book *Onward* that "Starbucks' coffee is exceptional, yes, but emotional connection is our true value proposition."[5] He was dismayed that this subtle concept was lost on some analysts and investors who were unable to appreciate its power because they didn't share his vision or were simply cynical regarding the financial return on Starbucks's investment in emotion. Schultz was resolute in his vision for the company; his mantra became "Starbucks is not a coffee company that serves people. It is a people company that serves coffee."[6]

Airbnb exhibits a similar obsession with experience. The firm strives, above all, to create a feeling of belonging on the part of guests who stay in its rentals when traveling. Its goal is for customers to feel personal connections to the people renting them rooms and a deeper sense of belonging in the communities they are visiting. This emphasis is intended to overcome the "stranger/danger bias" that makes most people uncomfortable when staying in the home of someone they have never met (or, on the other side of the interaction, makes hosts uncomfortable renting rooms in their homes to people they don't know). Each action of Airbnb is designed to enhance the level of trust between guests and hosts.

Airbnb then goes one step further. It thinks of its own culture in terms of experience—seeking to enhance the feeling of belonging and community within its own ranks. It takes its customer

experience mantra and looks at its own culture and, more generally, way of operating.[7] The firm wants its customers to have a per-
sonalized experience in terms of the types of rentals they want, the
neighborhoods they want to stay in, and even the types of hosts
they prefer. The focus to date has been primarily on the types of
rentals, but the company is developing approaches to help guests
find neighborhoods and hosts that fit their preferences. It is now
doing the same with its employees, looking at how to provide them
with what they need to make working at the firm a memorable experience. Airbnb is trying not just to shape what its people think
("we work together to create a great sense of community") but,
more importantly, it wants to shape what they feel as a result of
the experiences they have within the company. This perspective
has led to a deliberate set of choices in regard to all things that
touch employees. The firm's head of employee experience (who as-
sumes the responsibilities of a traditional human resources leader
and more) leads a team that is dedicated to creating memorable
experiences for Airbnb employees. Every point of connection that
an employee has with the company is examined and improved
with this goal in mind (including functions such as recruiting,
training, facilities, people development, compensation and benefits, and communication). One example of the firm's emphasis on
enhancing experience is how it manages its hiring process. The
team responsible for this process delineated each "touch point" in
the Airbnb interactions with potential hires and sought to make
them as positive as possible. This included a personal acknowl-
edgement of each application, regular updates on the status of the
application, suggestions on how they can learn about the company,
a process to welcome and integrate those who are accepted, and an
offer for someone in the firm to speak to those who are rejected to
provide feedback and encouragement.[8] The emphasis on experience also impacts life at the Airbnb headquarters building, where
people can work in any location they prefer (for example, the conference room, library, or cafeteria) or work remotely. The firm's
founders, two of whom are graduates of design school, even took

pains to create conference rooms that more fully engage people. One had an idea when walking by an IKEA furniture store and seeing an area set up like a room to show potential buyers what its furniture would look like in their own homes. He wondered what it would feel like to have a meeting in that room—wouldn't it be more interesting, more fun, and more productive than sitting in the boring conference rooms found in most corporations? At the Airbnb headquarters in San Francisco, each conference room is a nearly exact replica of an Airbnb rental somewhere in the world. Attend a meeting at Airbnb and you may be working in a room that replicates one of its apartment rentals in Paris. Or you may find yourself in a replica of Frank Sinatra's former home in Palm Springs, which is also a listing on the Airbnb website. At most firms, you find photographs of the firm's products or customers in the lobbies or on conference room walls—Airbnb, as in many areas, goes one step further.

The company also provides a range of benefits, including free gourmet food three times a day. It is puppy friendly, allowing its employees to bring their dogs to the office. Each employee receives $2,000 a year to stay in Airbnb rentals anywhere in the world when on vacation. As with the conference room design, the company wants its employees to stay connected to its customers, and giving them money to stay in its rentals promotes that goal.

Airbnb's focus on experience recently resulted in it displacing Google as the highest rated "great place to work" on an annual survey conducted by the career website Glassdoor (with the results based on employee input).[9] Airbnb's CEO Brian Chesky, on the same survey, received a 97 percent favorable rating from those working in the company. Airbnb's obsession with enhancing experience suggests that the culture of every firm should be viewed through the lens of experience and, more directly, the emotions that people have as a result of working in a company. This mandate becomes even more important when we realize that many people view the workplace as second only to their homes as a central place in their lives. Some, in fact, view the workplace as the most important place in their lives—more important than their family homes.[10] The key idea is that, like a great product, the feeling that people have about their company, how they emotionally respond to it, is more important than what they think about it.

⚡

Culture, then, is a combination of cognitive assumptions and emotional experiences. Cutting-edge groups pay attention to both, but most notable is their focus on the emotional side of company life and, in particular, the experiences that shape those emotions. Zappos and Whole Foods are highly visible in their efforts to create an optimistic and happy company culture. Alibaba's founder, Jack Ma, doesn't want to hear people in his company complain—instead, he wants them to take responsibility to act on improving those things that need to be improved. Support for this approach comes from Kim Cameron, a professor at the University of Michigan, who studies the impact of sentiments on company performance.[11] He found, overall, that firms that create positive work environments have better results. He defines a positive environment as one where people provide support to one another, avoid placing blame when things go wrong, and treat each other with gratitude and respect. He suggests that these sentiments produce better outcomes because they increase people's ability to work collaboratively, think creatively, and bounce back from adversity.

Emotions, of course, are both positive and negative. Cutting-edge firms also manage the negative emotions of team life. The leaders of Pixar, for example, believe that experimentation in the making of its films is essential if it is to remain creatively vital—avoiding the trap of only repeating what worked in the past. However, experimentation always raises the possibility of failure in that new ideas and practices often don't work. Intellectually, people understand the learning that comes from failure, but the emotions of failing are still problematic. Their minds tell them to try something new, but their guts say that failure is painful and should be avoided. As a result, Pixar strives to create a level of psychological safety that allows directors and their teams to be willing to try new things.[12] They do this through a variety of actions, but the most important is the support given to directors by the senior leadership of the firm. That support has limits, as noted earlier, but goes further and deeper than what one finds at most conventional companies.

✗

One reason why culture provides a competitive advantage is that it can't easily be replicated. The fact that culture is difficult to build and sustain is what makes it valuable. Those firms that get it right realize how hard it is for other firms to do the same. Competitors can't simply mandate what people should think and feel ("We will start, beginning next month, caring more about our employees."). Jack Ma, the founder of Alibaba, knows that many firms want to compete with his firm and emulate its practices. He tells them that they will fail because they don't realize the effort required to get culture right—through recruiting the right people, training them in the core values of the company, developing formal and informal processes that reinforce cultural traits, and taking action on those who violate its norms. Ma spent 10 years shaping his firm's culture and believes that those who want to replicate his success often lack the creativity and commitment needed to do the same.

Culture change is difficult for at least two reasons. First, culture evolves from what worked in the past for a particular firm and its leaders. In some cases, core cultural values go back decades and are linked to the beliefs and behavior of a firm's founders. For example, a firm that thrived as a result of aggressive financial management will have difficulty changing that belief and its associated practices, even when its market share is eroding due to inferior products or poor customer service. Financial engineering produced success at an early point in its growth cycle and is part of the firm's DNA. Culture, viewed in this light, is not an irrational set of beliefs and emotions but instead the embodiment of practices that become institutionalized as a result of past success. Cultures reflect what produced positive results and even when those practices are outdated, people are resistant to leave them behind. Even more challenging is the fact that most cultures have a taken-for-granted quality that makes it difficult for insiders to understand and change what needs changing. It is often newcomers, those experiencing a culture for the first time, who see things that need to change that others no longer notice.

The second challenge in changing culture is that one size doesn't fit all. What is right for one firm may not be right for another firm. What works at Netflix will not work at Zappos. Those seeking to develop the right culture can't simply mimic the values or practices of other companies or teams—they can learn from them, but each company needs to develop, and refine over time, a set of cultural norms that fit its specific needs. Many firms, for example, want to help their people manage the professional and personal demands on their time. Most cutting-edge firms give their people greater flexibility in the hours they work (with a few exceptions, such as the need to attend key meetings or work set hours for those in customer-facing groups). Pixar promotes this type of flexibility, in part, by keeping its headquarters open 24 hours a day, seven days a week. It realizes that some employees prefer to work off-hours and encourages them to work times that are best for them. Patagonia, in contrast, locks the doors of its headquarters at 8 p.m. every night and over weekends. It wants its people to take time away from work and recharge. Both firms are doing what they believe is in the best interests of their employees but take very different approaches. Which is correct? That depends. The experience of working in a building that is open all hours may feel right and positive to Pixar employees. But that same approach may feel hypocritical to Patagonia employees (given the firm's emphasis on taking time outside of work to play and experience nature). In developing culture, there is no cookbook—each firm needs to chart its own path. Jack Ma put it this way: "You should learn from your competitor, but never copy. Copy and you die."[13]

𝒩

A dramatic case of culture change occurred at Disney Animation. When Disney bought Pixar in 2006, it gave Pixar's leadership control over its studio. It was a reverse acquisition of sorts in that the acquired studio (Pixar) took control of the acquiring studio. Disney Animation, which achieved iconic status under the leadership of its famous founder, was no longer a pacesetter in its industry. In fact, it was producing what were charitably described as forgettable films that failed artistically and commercially. One veteran of the Disney studio noted, "I can't pinpoint where we lost our way, but it was affected by the fact that the people in charge weren't necessarily lovers of the art form."[14] In this case, the positive elements of the culture created by Walt Disney were not passed on to the next generation of leadership.

The new leaders took several months to assess what was ailing Disney Animation—observing how the studio operated and listening to people from all levels about what was needed to bring the company back to life. In particular, they were interested in what they called the "psychology and sociology" of how the studio operated. Their first major decision involved structure. Some within the company and externally wanted to combine the two studios, which, in essence, would mean that Disney Animation would be consumed within the more successful Pixar studio. John Lasseter and Ed Catmull, Pixar's leaders, took a contrarian position and decided that the best course of action was to keep the two studios separate. They wanted to preserve the history and identity of each group. Disney, founded in 1923, was responsible for creating movies based on hand-drawn animation whereas Pixar literally invented computer animation. Each studio needed to evolve with the introduction of new tools and techniques but remain true to its heritage. The leaders went one step further and limited how much employees from one studio could interact with or influence those in the other studio (by restricting who could attend meetings in each group and the roles they could play when they did attend those meetings). Their intent was to ensure that Pixar sustained the culture that had produced a string of successful films, such as *Toy Story*, while Disney found its way back to the glory days of classic films such as *Snow White*. The goal was not to make Disney a replica of Pixar—the goal was to make Disney more like Disney.

The new leaders then took what they learned over two decades at Pixar and made selective changes at Disney. They started by assessing whether Disney's decline was due to a talent deficiency. They determined that the creative staff at Disney was not the problem. Most of these individuals were highly skilled and dedicated to their craft. However, the executives running the studio lacked a passion for animation and great storytelling. "None of them grew up wanting to create animation. None of them," a Pixar leader noted. "Those are the people we let go." The next step was to form a group they called the *Brain Trust* to get the studio's films on track. This group, consisting of people with deep experience in the making of successful films, is designed to review films in progress. The Brain Trust meeting starts with a review of a film in progress, followed by a candid and often intense give and take regarding what is working and what is not. Suggested changes that surface in the meeting are not forced on the film's director, but the feedback must be taken seriously. The director of the hit Disney movie *Frozen* noted about these meetings, "Sometimes you come out very tired, but you never come out of it feeling like you don't know what to do or where to go."[15]

Another change designed to revitalize the studio was to upgrade the look and feel of the Disney building, with an emphasis on individual creativity. Ed Catmull, CEO of Pixar, describes how surprised he was during his first visit to the Disney Animation headquarters to find such a sterile environment—everything in its place, each desk clean and orderly, people exceedingly polite and professional. He mentioned this to his host for the day and was told that people in the studio wanted to make a good impression on him during his visit. Catmull and Lasseter quickly signaled that a creative company must not look, or act, like an accounting firm. They created a central gathering place, called the Caffeine Patch, which was decorated in what can best be described as a childlike environment full of colorful animated characters and posters from the most recent Disney films. The resulting space was one that a 10-year-old would love. The members of the studio were also encouraged to decorate their own work areas as they saw fit—the more colorful and quirkier the better. The intent of these actions by the new leadership was to build a creative community of people who shared a passion for their films and a responsibility for making them great.

✦

Each cutting-edge firm believes it is unique. These firms say as much on their websites and in their public statements. The firms profiled in this book are clearly different than traditional firms but are also different from each other—as noted in regard to the culture of each firm:

Culture Themes in Cutting-Edge Firms [16]

COMPANY	CULTURE THEMES ABOUT THEIR WORKING ENVIRONMENT
Alibaba	*Hupan Spirit:* Embody the startup mentality evident when the firm was founded—with an emphasis on a shared passion for the work and an intense drive to succeed.
Airbnb	*Belonging:* Foster a feeling of community and connection among employees. Enhance the experience of those who work in the company.
Netflix	*Freedom and Responsibility:* Hire great people, surround them with great colleagues, and allow them to operate as they see fit. Then hold them accountable for results.
Patagonia	*Work Hard, Play Hard:* Bring together a group of nature-loving, iconoclastic "dirt bags" who share a passion for their work and play.
Pixar	*Creativity Through Collaboration:* Foster a creative community of people who share a deep commitment to their craft and each other.
Whole Foods	*Democratic Discipline:* Give people a strong voice in how the company is run while embracing a robust set of performance-enhancing practices.
Zappos	*Deliver Happiness:* Enhance the happiness of each member of the Zappos family.

Contrast the cultural themes noted with what you find in many firms, whose cultures are so generic, so bland, that you could easily take the principles from one and apply them to another ("we focus on our customers and their needs," "integrity is key to everything we do," "quality is nonnegotiable," "teamwork is the key to our success"). While noting the idiosyncratic nature of cutting-edge firms, we can also stand back and ask, at a deeper level, how are the cultures of these cutting-edge companies alike? What are the similarities in the experiences and emotions of people working within these firms and their teams?

The Look and Feel of Cutting-Edge Cultures

	CUTTING-EDGE COMPANIES AND TEAMS	INEFFECTIVE COMPANIES AND TEAMS
All In	Deeply committed to the firm's purpose, values and success; act with a high level of energy and ambition to make a difference	A job is a job; lack of ownership and engagement; low energy
Autonomous	Have the autonomy and authority needed to make decisions on how to achieve the group's goals; flat organizational structure	Top-down control and monitoring of people's goals, work process, and decisions; formal chain of command
Transparent	Know what is expected in regard to performance and behavior; company and leaders share information in an open and authentic manner	Secretive culture with little sharing of information; communication spin from senior leaders is the norm

	CUTTING-EDGE COMPANIES AND TEAMS	**INEFFECTIVE COMPANIES AND TEAMS**
Accountable	Take full responsibility for the way they work and their performance; team-level rewards for superior performance and consequences for poor performance	Vague performance goals; lack of ownership for subpar performance; few team rewards for superior performance
Playful	Find pleasure in the work itself; enjoy interacting with colleagues	Low-energy workplace; cynicism about a company's vision, culture, and leaders
Communal	Share a sense of community and a willingness to help others; high levels of trust	Cold and bureaucratic environment; pervasive distrust; self-serving behavior

The cutting-edge firms in this book embrace, in various ways, each of the listed cultural attributes. One company will emphasize some of these attributes more than others, but each has elements of all six. Netflix, for example, models the harder side of cutting-edge cultures (with its emphasis on accountability) while Zappos models the softer side (with its emphasis on a playful work environment). Determining the cultural traits that your company or team needs is a first necessary step in creating the right culture for your firm or team—but only a first step. Culture is created by practices and behaviors that foster the desired assumptions and emotions. These actions, not a firm's statements of intent, require a high level of commitment and creativity on the part of a firm and, in particular, its leadership.

All In

Airbnb goes to great lengths to make work meaningful for its employees. First, it is an ideologically driven company with a larger purpose of creating trust and belonging in communities around the world. This "higher calling" taps into the needs of many people, millennials and otherwise, to work for a company that contributes to society. Second, Airbnb provides its people with a great deal of say in the projects on which they want to work. Members of the company can change projects depending on their interests and talents. While this doesn't occur on a regular basis because continuity is important in finishing projects, staff and their supervisors will initiate changes that ensure the highest level of employee engagement with the work itself. A third element of making work meaningful at Airbnb is the attention paid to the work environment. The company wants people to feel fully supported in their work and connected to their coworkers—which includes a wide variety of company policies and practices designed to achieve that goal. The company hires "true believers" and then goes to great lengths to support them in pursuing the work that matters.

Patagonia is also a purpose-driven firm—but not in regard to growth or sales. Patagonia's goal is to be a company that can survive for 100 years or longer, which the firm's leaders believe requires a more moderate growth rate. Its primary purpose is lessening the impact that people and companies have on the environment. It recently sponsored a study examining the impact of the synthetic fibers used in its fleece jackets on the health of the Earth's oceans and rivers. The findings suggest that the tiny specs of plastic shed from synthetic clothing when washed can be potentially dangerous to our public waterways. Patagonia, consistent with its mission and culture, is making the study's findings public and will determine how it and other manufactures can minimize the resulting environmental damage. Patagonia is also sponsoring lower-tech initiatives, such as its Worn Wear program that encourages people to repair or recycle its clothing (versus discarding it and buying more clothing). This program has a vehicle, a recycled 1991 Dodge truck that runs on biofuel, that goes cross country, stopping at various locations—Patagonia retail stores, farmers markets, state parks, and coffee shops—providing free clothing repairs and environmental workshops.

Autonomous

Whole Foods's highly decentralized approach is based on the belief that those closest to the customers are in the best position to make decisions on how to best serve those customers. The company also believes innovation is more likely when it begins at a local level and is then adopted by others if successful. The Whole Foods in Sonoma, California, was the first to have a Wine Bar. Venice, California, was the first to have a kombucha tea bar. Dallas, Texas, was the first to have a spa, including the option of having employees shop for customers as they receive treatments. Augusta, Georgia, home of the Masters golf tournament, was the first to have a putting green at the facility. None of these experiments were mandated or even suggested by the firm's corporate office. These local experiments are in addition to larger-scale changes that the company is making to attract new customers. It is, for example, inviting outside vendors to lease space in its new brand of stores, called 365. The goal is to attract younger, more price-sensitive shoppers with lower costs and a range of customized products.

Netflix is another firm built on the idea that people and teams must be free to determine how to go about their jobs. The company strives to hire extraordinarily talented people who want to have an impact—and then gives them the autonomy needed to achieve their goals. In particular, the firm doesn't want process to be viewed as a substitute for people performing at a high level. It believes that the most talented people want to work in an environment that provides them with a great deal of independence and doesn't dictate how they work. The company thus asks, "Do we really need this process? Isn't there a simpler way that makes everyone's life easier?" The goal, in short, is to have as few mandated processes and policies as possible. The few rules that remain in place are intended to prevent a catastrophe (such as the theft of customer credit card information) or people breaking the law (such as workplace harassment).[17] To fight against what it describes as "rule creep," Netflix doesn't just simplify its work processes and administrative requirements—it does away with them whenever possible. It eliminated, for example, the reporting of vacation time by its employees.[18] Each person determines the timing and duration of his or her vacation and then discusses it with his or her supervisor to avoid any confusion. Netflix also did away with detailed expense guidelines (such as airfare or hotel restrictions). It simply asks its employees to spend money as if it were their own. The firm's expense policy is, "Act in Netflix's best interests." Another example is the elimination of performance reviews within the firm, which were replaced with ongoing supervisor/ employee discussions combined with periodic peer feedback that asks what each person should stop, start, or continue. Some of these 360-degree reviews are even done in person, where a small group of people meet with an individual to provide feedback. The senior human resources leader at the company when these changes were made, Patty McCord, noted that "building a bureaucracy and elaborate rituals around measuring performance usually doesn't improve it."[19]

Transparent

Whole Foods is one of the most transparent firms in the world in sharing a wide range of information with its employees. The company, operating with an "open book" approach, makes available to everyone the performance results for each team, each store, and the company in total. The norm in the company is to share as much as possible, both in terms of performance data and the reasons behind its key decisions. The firm's CEO, John Mackey, explains why it is so committed to sharing information:

> The high-trust organization takes the risk of revealing too much information. We must be willing to take the risk that some valuable information may fall into the wrong hands because our commitment to empowerment and trust necessitates taking that risk. Creating transparency and authentic communication is an ongoing challenge that every organization faces. We must continually strive to remove the barriers that prevent it, knowing that we can't maintain high levels of organizational trust without transparency and authentic communication.[20]

Transparency is also important at Netflix, but it is less about data and metrics—and more about straight talk regarding where the company stands and what needs to be done to achieve its goals. A pivotal point occurred early in its history when expenditures exceeded sales. One-third of the workforce was let go, and those remaining were told the harsh truth about the company's vulnerable financial position. The leaders of Netflix believe that people are aware of when their leaders are lying to them or spinning the truth in regard to performance, a key decision, or even an employee's standing within the firm. As a result, Netflix strives to be very direct in how it communicates with its people. For example, new hires are told, in their first orientation session, that the company is not a family but a team—and successful teams upgrade talent whenever possible. People are told that they will not be with the firm if they don't perform at a high level. They are also told that they should obtain information regarding their value in the marketplace (based on competitive salaries) and then engage in discussions with the supervisor and the human resources department regarding that information. The company wants to pay people based on market conditions, and that information is helpful.

Accountable

Netflix emphasizes that people and teams are fully accountable for the results they produce. If people prove unworthy of the freedom they are provided, based on a lack of performance, they are given a generous severance package. If someone stumbles and fails to perform, he or she is given time to recover—but not too much time.[21] Accountability, at Netflix, means that effort, hard work, and past performance are largely irrelevant in assessing performance. This can be a tough reality for some people, but Netflix doesn't try to accommodate them. Instead, the company seeks to hire those who can thrive in its culture and keep out, or remove, those who can't perform with it. In the firm's culture presentation, this approach is summarized as follows:

Netflix: Our High Performance Culture is Not Right for Everyone

➡ Many people love our culture, and stay a long time—they thrive on excellence and candor and change—they would be disappointed if given a severance package, their relationship with Netflix is marked by mutual warmth and respect

➡ Some people, however, value job security and stability over performance, and don't like our culture—They feel fearful at Netflix—They are sometimes bitter if let go, and feel that we are a political place to work

➡ We're getting better at attracting only the former, and helping the latter realize we are not right for them[22]

Zappos has a softer culture than Netflix, but it has developed creative ways to ensure that people are accountable. For example, Zappos places great emphasis on customer service and, more generally, customer happiness (what it calls WOW). The company tracks a variety of statistics such as the number of calls handled, which its call-center people see every day. However, Zappos doesn't set targets on call time or upsell revenue. The key metric is what the company calls the Personal Emotional Connection. This is assessed several times a week by staff who listen in on calls and assess the effectiveness of call-center members. Their ratings are shared with each person and improvement areas are discussed. Another key metric is what it calls a Net Promoter Score. This metric compares the number of people, as assessed by a follow-up survey, who recommend or promote Zappos to others versus those who are detractors of the company. This metric is tracked each day, and the company posts the scores for customers who fill out the survey.

Playful

Alibaba culture can appear strange to those who are accustomed to a more formal corporate environment. The firm acts like a large family where people connect in a manner that you don't find in many corporations. Ma, for example, wants his people to take on kung fu nicknames upon joining the firm, names that fit their personalities. His nickname means "unpredictable and aggressive."[23] Ma believes people should feel playfully engaged by their company and its leaders. He is comfortable acting out at Alibaba's corporate gatherings—one year, he dressed liked Lady Gaga and sang pop songs to 15,000 of his cheering employees. He has conducted informal ceremonies blessing hundreds of Alibaba newlyweds, who are dressed in full wedding garb, at the firm's annual company event. Such actions cause some to call him "Crazy Jack"—the man who founded a company that is on course to become the first trillion-dollar business in the world.

Zappos, much like Alibaba, thinks that play, including an element of weirdness, is good for business. Take, for example, the celebratory events that the company sponsors almost continuously to increase the level of happiness that its people experience at work. Over the span of several months this year, Zappos held the following fun events:

→ Celebrated Saint Patrick's Day with a contest to determine the employee with the best kilt, along with live music and green beer.

→ Recognized Pi Day (3.14) with a pie-eating contest. The winner finished off two pies in five minutes without the use of his hands.

→ Hosted a concert in the headquarters building featuring the band Mercy Music.

→ Provided a day off for all employees on Leap Day (2/29). They were encouraged to use the day to check off something on their bucket lists. CEO Tony Hsieh spent the day officiating the wedding between two of his employees. The ceremony took place at the trailer park where Hsieh lives, with many members of the Zappos family, along with his two pet alpacas, in attendance.

→ Sponsored a Chinese New Year festival in its headquarters plaza, with singing, a dragon-blessing ceremony, and musical performances.[24]

In looking at the "playful" side of the leaders of each firm in this book, we see that most if not all of them are quite different than a typical corporate leader. Consider that John Mackey of Whole Foods took off six months from his role as co-CEO to hike the Appalachian Trail. Or that Patagonia's founder, Yvon Chouinard, now 73, continues to engage in risky outdoor activities.[25]

Communal

Pixar believes in the need to create a sense community within a company. This results in an environment where people are more inclined to help each other. One employee noted, "Of great importance—and something that sets us apart from other studios, is the way people at all levels support one another. Everyone is fully invested in helping everyone else turn out the best work. They really do feel that it's all for one and one for all."[26] A director at the studio, Dan Scanlon, adds,

> Sometimes those films go through some dark phases, where they're really not working, and it's important to have someone like John who always goes back to the beginning. When things aren't working, he says, "When we came up with the idea for this, I heard this thing, and the heart that's in there. I know that that's still there." . . . . "You're responsible for your mistakes, but there's no blame culture. As a freelancer in London, I knew that if I'd made a critical error, I'd be out of a job. Here, they'd say you have to learn from it, and strive to do better. It's the most grown up place I've ever worked in that regard. It's all about ownership.[27]

Community, at least at Pixar, also helps with the open exchange of ideas across group boundaries. Pixar believes that people in different groups need to interact on a regular basis. Steve Jobs, who bought what became Pixar from George Lucas, insisted on the firm's building having a common area that would force interaction among people from different functional teams. As a result, the building is designed in a way that pulls people out of their offices and functional areas into centrally located spaces—a company restaurant, coffee bar, mailboxes, and restrooms. Jobs believed that these personal interactions, even if brief, are essential if a firm is to cross-pollinate new ideas and share the lessons people are learning. The Pixar building design is just the most visible element of its belief in fostering a community where ideas flow easily across boundaries. It has, for example, a norm that anyone in the company can engage anyone else with ideas or requests—there is no need to go through what in many firms is a formal chain of command. This norm came about in reaction to the negative experience of one of the firm's founders when he worked at Disney 20 years earlier. In that culture, people needed to ask for permission from their supervisor before they could approach other departments—which resulted in a rigid culture where people were more concerned with protecting their own areas of authority than collaborating to make a great film. Pixar, in contrast, emphasizes that all people should feel free to express their ideas on any aspect of a film as it progresses. Catmull underscores the importance of culture in Pixar's success:

> If we get that right, the result is a vibrant community where talented people are loyal to one another and their collective work, everyone feels that they are part of something extraordinary, and their passion and accomplishments make the community a magnet for talented people coming out of schools or working at other places.[28]

Zappos, with 1,500 employees and an estimated $2 billion in revenue, has many communal cultural traits. On its website, it notes,

> We are more than just a team though—we are a family. We watch out for each other, care for each other, and go above and beyond for each other because we believe in each other and we trust each other. We work together, but we also play together. Our bonds go far beyond the typical "co-worker" relationships found at most other companies.[29]

The company's goal is to enhance happiness—first for customers, but also for employees. That purpose influences who the firm hires and how they treat them once they join the firm. In its value statement, the firm makes this clear: "The best team members have a positive influence on one another and everyone they encounter. They strive to eliminate any kind of cynicism and negative interactions. They strive to create harmony with each other and with everyone else they come in contact with."[30]

Zappos does a number of things to promote a positive work environment. The firm's founders believe that bonds develop through personal interactions. As a result, employees are required to come into the office versus working remotely. The Zappos CEO notes, "We really wanted to build the company around culture, company culture being the number one priority. And it's much easier to build a culture when it's actually in person versus remotely by email."[31] The company also wants its people to spend time together socializing outside of work. Managers at Zappos are expected to spend upwards of 20 percent of their time outside of the office with their team members (at various social events that they host or attend). Zappos learned early in its history that a number of people applying for managerial positions don't believe in socializing outside of the office, which was a problem in a company that views itself as a close-knit family. Zappos views this as nonnegotiable and does not hire people who want to keep their work and personal lives separate.

Zappos also uses technology in a creative manner to foster closer relationships among its people. It uses technology in what they call the *Face Game* to encourage connections among people. Those logging onto company computers are shown photos of other employees and asked if they know the people's names. After responding, they are shown the person's job profile. People are scored on their ability to identify others as they log on, with higher scores indicating a more connected individual. The company also looks at the Face Game data in aggregate to understand the networks across the company at a group level (with some groups or functions being more connected than others and the impact those connections have on the business).

✎

Culture influences the way we view our environments, what we hold to be important, and how we go about our day-to-day work. David Foster Wallace, the novelist, makes the point that life in general often has a taken-for-granted quality to it. He suggests that this human tendency is something we need to fight—being careful to not simply go into what he called "default mode," where we jump to quick conclusions about what is occurring around us. Wallace's insight also applies to the cultures of our organizations and teams. He uses a simple parable to convey his point:

> There are these two young fish swimming along, and they happen to meet an older fish swimming the other way, who nods at them and says, "Morning, boys, how's the water?" And the two young fish swim on for a bit, and then eventually one of them looks over at the other and goes, "What the hell is water?"[32]

Wallace's point is that that which surrounds us is often the very thing we can't see, question, or even discuss. In essence, people stop seeing that which is all around them. Cutting-edge firms and their teams are notable in being more aware of culture and more deliberate in what they want, and don't want, in those cultures. They articulate what is important and continually debate the degree to which they are acting in a manner consistent with their particular beliefs and values. The lesson from these firms and teams is the need to question one's own culture, along with a relentless commitment to getting it right.

 **TAKEAWAYS**

> ➤ Cutting-edge firms establish a distinctive "hard/soft" culture by first clarifying the attributes and emotions that they want in their companies. The don't mimic other firms.

> ➤ They then develop formal and informal mechanisms to reinforce those attributes. In particular, they identify the

experience they want their employees to have as a result of working in the company.

➤ The result is that members know what is expected of them—what to do, what not to do—what is valued and, what is taboo.

CHAPTER

6

TAKE COMFORT IN DISCOMFORT

Tell Me Something I Don't Want to Hear[1]

Alibaba was founded almost two decades ago by a charismatic, some would say eccentric, leader named Jack Ma. He enlisted 17 of his friends to pursue an audacious goal—Ma wanted to dominate the emerging Chinese e-commerce marketplace and then expand globally. Alibaba initially focused on promoting business-to-business transactions between international buyers and Chinese manufacturers. Its goal was to help small- and medium-sized businesses in China gain access to global markets. After several years of strong growth, Alibaba opened a second Internet site serving retail customers in China. In so doing, it saw itself as going to war with a much larger and more well-established competitor—eBay. Alibaba did this because Ma believed that eBay would eventually come after his firm's business-to-business customers. Alibaba decided that the best defense was a strong offense.

Ma didn't launch a massive company-wide effort to develop a competitive consumer website. Instead, he selected six of his people to work on the secret project—an assignment that they could not share with anyone in the company or even with their families. They were then "quarantined," working, and often living, in the original apartment in which Alibaba had been born just a few years earlier. The team's mandate was to develop an Internet auction site that better met the needs and preferences of Chinese consumers and, in so doing, displace eBay—then the most successful e-commerce firm in the world. Ma liked the idea of his small team going into battle against eBay—framing it as David versus Goliath. He was placing his firm's future in the hands of six dedicated people striving to achieve an audacious goal.[2] His faith was well placed.[3] Several years later, after spending $250 million and putting its reputation on the line, eBay pulled out of China.[4] The rise of Alibaba captured people's attention—an unknown startup in Communist China had found a way to defeat a Silicon Valley icon that had more money, better technology, and a clear plan of action.[5]

Alibaba pushed forward and expanded into a number of adjacent businesses, such as Alipay, which provides PayPal-like financial services customized to the Chinese market, and AliCloud, which provides Amazon-like cloud computing services. The company now has 25 business units, 38,000 employees, and over 370 million active customers—more customers than people living in the United States. It is China's largest retailer, offering almost anything a consumer could want—from clothing, to groceries, to automobiles.[6] It is the source of more than 60 percent of the packages shipped through the Chinese postal system.[7] The next step for Alibaba, using the capital from its recent public offering, is accelerating its push into new geographical markets such as India and Brazil.[8]

The extraordinary success of Alibaba couldn't have happened without a number of strategic and operational wins. The Chinese government, for example, supported Alibaba's growth by giving it exclusive rights in areas such as Alipay (which allowed the company to offer financial services that were critical in building customer trust and loyalty). The mistakes of its primary competitor also helped. eBay had a short-term focus on being a public company, facing pressure to justify its massive investment in the Chinese market. eBay was also hindered by its desire to replicate what worked in the United States in the Chinese market. For example, eBay wanted its Chinese operation to operate from the same technology platform as its legacy U.S. group. Once that change occurred, it was reported that it took nine weeks to change even one word on the Chinese eBay website due to the resulting bureaucracy. At Alibaba, such changes could be made in just hours, which allowed it to more effectively respond to changing customer and market conditions.[9] Beyond these factors, we must still ask, how did Alibaba achieve such extraordinary results?

One factor in Alibaba's success was hiring the right people. It sought out those with an entrepreneurial streak who act with "fire in the belly" and "never give up on doing what they believe is right."[10] The company, like many startups, looked for those who were similar in temperament to its founding members. Jack Ma believes such people are valuable because they had to struggle for their success in life—they have a few nicks and scars. He hired people who were one or two levels below the best students in their universities. He thinks those at the top of their classes would not have the resilience needed to withstand the setbacks that come with operating in a tough marketplace like China, where failure is common. Ma also believes that people with impressive resumes often have problems bonding with others because they feel superior given their success. As a result, they often fail to work in a collaborative manner with their colleagues, which comprises the spirit of teamwork within the company. Ma is fond of saying that a good team, one with a clear focus and operating as a cohesive family, can defeat a competitor 10 times its size.

Ma's defining leadership trait is his passion—he operates with a high level of enthusiasm and resolve. He expects the same from members of his teams. The result is a demanding work environment where people work long and passionate hours. In particular, Alibaba encourages intense debate among colleagues, viewing conflict as inevitable and productive. Its leaders have no problem if shouting matches break out during company meetings. In fact, Alibaba views combative behavior, what it calls *quarrelling*, among team members as a sign that they want to "excel from the bottom of their heart" and achieve "critical execution."[11] An insider who worked in the firm writes about its culture, "Alibaba is not a group of civilised gentlemen, or men who nicely play by the rules. They are reckless with ambition, they are radical and aggressive. Everyone walks out of a meeting room beet-red from shouting, that's how we held meetings—with our voices raised. It's very intense."[12] This doesn't mean that anything goes at Alibaba—people can't attack others on a personal level. But they are expected to aggressively attack their ideas if there is a better idea. Ma believes that most large companies stumble because they develop what he calls a "little white rabbit" culture. In these firms, people get along well but don't challenge each other. As a result, performance suffers and the firm slowly declines.

Alibaba's approach to teamwork differs from what is found in many corporations—where people view intense conflict, especially in meetings, as a sign of trouble. These firms fear that conflict will inhibit people's ability to develop a solution that everyone can support and effectively execute. As a result, the emphasis is people behaving in a highly collaborative, even polite, manner. Conflicts are addressed through one-on-one discussions outside of the team meetings or through lobbying efforts to the team's leader (who then weighs competing arguments and makes a decision for the group). While this approach is sometimes appropriate, it becomes dysfunctional when conflicts can't be openly surfaced, discussed, and resolved in a team setting. In cutting-edge groups, a good meeting is one where a healthy fight results in a healthy outcome. In more conventional firms, a good meeting is one where people get along and everyone agrees on the best path forward. Conflict is viewed as a sign that the team is not working well. This is not to say that outcomes don't matter in more traditional firms, but the ability of people to work as a cohesive team, the willingness of people to be team players, can take priority over everything else—including results.

Irving Goffman, a sociologist, examined the informal rules that dominate social interactions. One of the most powerful determinants of people's behavior is what he calls *face saving*.[13] Goffman uses the term *face* to indicate how people in every culture create roles for themselves, particularly when in a public or group setting. Some people, for instance, want to be seen as the technical experts while others want to be seen as the most creative individuals on their teams. Goffman suggests that people become emotionally invested in these roles and look for support from others to affirm how they want to view themselves. Challenges to a person's role produce anxiety in that person and, in many cases, larger problems for the group due to the resulting interpersonal tensions. To avoid this, people will often act in ways that support another's self-perceptions and, more generally, their standing within a company or team. This often takes the form of polite norms of behavior, with the goal that everyone can "save face" when interacting with others. The unspoken norm is that I will reinforce the role you want to play if you reinforce the role that I want to play.

We can extrapolate from Goffman's idea and see that the most basic role, one that cuts across more specific roles, is that of being a valued team member. Being a member of a group matters a great deal to most people, and, inversely, they fear being ostracized by the group. In a business setting, being accepted means that one's ideas and actions are seen as helpful and contributing to the team's success. Face saving, in this more general sense, is the feeling of being valued by others as a team member.

Team members who are honest in expressing their views run the risk of breaking the face-saving norm. By challenging others, they risk exposing the flaws in others' thinking and, more generally, undermining their standing as respected members of the team. The more direct and assertive challenges can be felt as personal attacks by other team members, jeopardizing interpersonal relationship as well as the esprit de corps within the group. I have worked with teams where people hold grudges, in some cases for years, against those who publicly challenged them in a group setting. The downside of face-saving behavior is that people are less direct regarding their views on issues critical to the team's success. One could argue that face saving, while understandable, creates more harm than good because team members avoid saying what needs to be said.

Ursula Burns, on becoming the CEO of Xerox, knew that revenue growth was the key priority for her company, one that had only recently flirted with bankruptcy. To achieve this goal, she believed her firm's culture had to change. In particular, Burns wanted people to be less patient with each other and more direct in expressing their views. She described the problem as one of "terminal niceness," where those who had worked together for decades were loath to criticize each another, even if it involved an important strategic or operational threat. Burns, talking about the closeness of what she calls the Xerox family, wants her people to be more like what she views as a real family—one where people are direct and even tough because they care so much about each other.[14] She notes, "When we're in the family, you don't have to be as nice as when you're outside of the family . . . I want us to stay civil and kind, but we have to be frank—and the reason we can be frank is because we are all in the same family."[15] She goes even further in saying that people in Xerox need be aggressive and even rude if needed to produce a better outcome for the company. This was especially important to Burns in relation to what was occurring in her leadership team meetings, where people often had concerns about what was being presented or recommended—but rather than surface those concerns in the meeting, they came to her in private and shared their views. The sobering fact is that Burns, after years of pushing for a more open and direct exchange of views within Xerox, still saw signs that the culture had not changed as much as needed.

Some people also avoid conflict for fear of embarrassing themselves if they are proven wrong, or fail to win support, after putting forward their ideas. Consequently, they remain silent or express themselves in such subtle ways that others misread their intent. In more extreme cases, people will wait to see where others stand on an issue before voicing their ideas. Some go one step further and say what they think their team leader, or those in the dominant coalition within their group, want to hear or will support. The team dynamic, in these situations, becomes one where people will say they value debate but also believe that the honest expression of one's views is risky to them. Richard Holbrook commented on this tendency in many of the teams he observed over his long career:

> [You want] . . . an open airing of views and opinions and suggestions upward, but once the policy is decided you want rigorous, disciplined implementation of it. And very often . . . the exact opposite happens. People sit in a room, they don't air their real differences, a false and sloppy consensus papers over those underlying differences, and they go back to their offices and continue to work at cross-purposes, even actively undermining each other.[16]

Leaders sometimes contribute to this dysfunctional pattern of behavior by stating that they want open dialogue when, in reality, they want their teams to agree with their own points of view and preferred plans of action. As a result, team members will often go through the motions of debating various points of view when they know the decisions will eventually come back to what their leaders want. The entire decision-making process, then, becomes a charade, where people appear to debate options but know that the decision has already been made by their group's leader.

There are teams, however, where the leader sincerely desires an open exchange of ideas but it simply doesn't happen. At Xerox, Burns believed this was the result of long-standing relationships within the firm, which resulted in an aversion to challenging others, particularly in-group meetings. Another reason that a team leader will not get an open expression of ideas is the personality of those on the team. Team members can bring a set of negative experiences from their past teams, when they were open and were punished for it. This influences how they view an open expression of ideas and a direct approach to conflict in their current teams. They may, for example, have spent time at a firm that was highly political and learned to be indirect or even secretive in expressing their views. More generally, they learned to distrust others and reveal as little as possible regarding their own views on key topics.

Brad Bird, who has directed several Pixar firms, believes that these types of people destroy the ability of a team to function at a higher level—regardless of what a leader wants. These are people who don't deal openly with their peers, and some even go one step further and undermine what the team is striving to accomplish. Bird believes that people with this personality type will not change their behavior, even when he makes an effort to create an open and healthy team culture. He notes, "Passive-aggressive people—people who don't show their colors in the group but then get behind the scenes and peck away—are poisonous. I can usually spot those people fairly soon and I weed them out."[17]

✎

Managing conflict within a team, however, is more complicated than removing those who can't operate in an open and intense environment. Team members are often on the receiving end of two messages regarding what is expected of them. These messages are conveyed in a variety of ways, sometimes subtle, from a team leader, peers, or even the organization in which they work. They are as follows:

1. You must put forward your honest point of view on the decisions we face as a group and offer clear recommendations that help move us forward. If you fail to do so, you are not adding value as a team member and are increasing the likelihood that we will fail to achieve our goals.

2. You must operate in a highly collaborative manner and support your peers. If you fail to do so, you are not being a team player and are undermining our ability to work together as a group to achieve our goals.

If a team member fails to do either of the above, he or she is less valued as a team member and can even be rejected by the group or the group's leader. In the social sciences, there is a well-known concept called the *double-bind*.[18] In its purest form, a double-bind occurs when people experience two conflicting messages that are inherently at odds with each other. These messages create confusion in those receiving them because responding to one of the messages will result in a negative outcome in the other. That is, acting on either message triggers a negative outcome—thus, there is no completely problem-free way to respond. Moreover, the contradiction in the two messages is not acknowledged as being a contradiction, and the person receiving the message can't remove himself or herself from the dilemma that it creates. Most people, when confronted with a double-bind, freeze and do nothing—as this feels like the safest thing to do given the situation in which they find themselves.

One can, of course, argue that the two messages noted above are not mutually exclusive—that each can be achieved without undermining the other. That is, people can be both assertive and cooperative and, in fact, this is what is needed for them to be effective.[19] In other words, the most effective team members can put forward a contrary point of view but do so in a manner that does not alienate others or undermine the collaborative ethos within the team. That is clearly the goal, and some individuals and teams manage this much better than others. But the conflict double-bind is always a constant threat hanging over a team.

N

The first task in creating a conflict-friendly culture, and overcoming the double-bind, is redefining what it means to be comfortable. In many groups, comfort implies a lack of conflict or tension among team members. Everyone gets along, and decisions are reached in a highly collaborative manner. In cutting-edge teams, this definition of comfort is turned on its head—rejected in favor of surfacing or even creating tension among team members. These teams don't want their members to be too comfortable because that means that they have settled for the status quo. It means that they are not pushing themselves to achieve a higher level of performance and innovation. Comfort, then, is redefined as accepting the need to be uncomfortable. A new director to Pixar was surprised when the firm hired him to produce a film soon after he suffered a highly visible failure in another studio. He noted that the leadership of Pixar told him,

> The only thing we're afraid of is complacency—feeling like we have it all figured out. We want you to come shake things up. We will give you a good argument if we think what you're doing doesn't make sense, but if you can convince us, we'll do things a different way.[20]

Cutting-edge firms, then, are committed to deliberately creating conflict to produce better outcomes. Most people, when asked, will say that they are open to conflict and understand the role it plays in producing better decisions. But that statement is quite different from being willing to suffer the pain that comes with conflict. Talking about the benefits of productive conflict doesn't mitigate the discomfort that accompanies it in most situations. It is not a stretch to say that many team members don't want to experience the pain of conflict even when they know it may be in their group's best interest. Knowing something and acting on it are two different things.

Cutting-edge firms understand the challenge of getting people to move toward conflict and not away from it. One way to describe this is increasing the level of discomfort that people in the team can tolerate—creating an environment that has a higher pain threshold than what is found in most conventional groups. They raise the level of "heat" in their interactions when needed in order to fully understand the complex dynamics and potential tradeoffs in the decisions they are making. Another way of saying this is that people in cutting-edge firms create the conditions that help people be comfortable with the discomfort that comes with conflict. Airbnb provides an example of a company that strives to create a positive work environment but one that values honest dialogue. When an internal survey suggested that they needed to improve in this area, one of the firm's leaders came up with a phrase to encourage more open conversations. He described it as the need to surface the "elephants, dead fish and vomit." In his mind, elephants are the "undiscussables" that everyone recognizes but doesn't talk about (at least in a public forum). Dead fish are the things that happened in the past that some people come back to over and over again. The vomit is an issue or concern that people want to get out of their systems. As you might imagine, classifying each type of communication might result in a difference of opinion within Airbnb—an elephant to one person can be a dead fish to another! However, the intent is clear—get to the issues on the table and, if possible, even inject a bit of humor into the process of doing so.[21]

Another approach to help people surface uncomfortable truths is to separate ideas from people. This is the notion that people are not their ideas and an attack on an idea is about the work and not about them.[22] Making a distinction between ideas and the person proposing those ideas helps people be less defensive when others find fault in their proposals or come forward with a better proposal. The distinction allows conflict to escalate to a higher level of intensity and be "pressure tested" and, in so doing, increases the likelihood of generating better ideas and solutions. The problem, of course, is that most people do identify with their ideas. In real life, ideas are always personal. This is particularly true when a team is comprised of passionate or even obsessive people. That said, the goal in cutting-edge groups is to direct people's passion toward creating the best work product—and away from defending themselves or their groups against what some may see as critics. The CEO of Pixar emphasizes the need for this in any creative enterprise:

> The film—not the filmmaker—is under the microscope. This principle eludes most people, but it is critical: You are not your idea, and if you identify too closely with your ideas, you will take offense when challenged. Andrew Stanton, who has been

on the giving or the receiving end of almost every Braintrust meeting we've had, likes to say that if Pixar were a hospital and the movies its patients, then the Braintrust is made up of trusted doctors. It's important to remember that the movie's director and producer are "doctors" too. It's as if they've gathered a panel of consulting experts to help find an accurate diagnosis for an extremely confounding case.[23]

A second task in effectively raising the level of discomfort within a team is setting bold, even audacious, goals. These goals are not designed to produce conflict, but conflict is almost always the result. Imagine being named the director of a new film at Pixar, a studio that has produced one blockbuster after another, one creative success after another. As a new director, you can take some comfort in the fact that the studio has developed a set of innovative technologies and processes that set it apart from other studios (such as providing feedback in a variety of well-established forums). But the creative element of making a Pixar film, which can take up to four years, is inevitably a journey into the unknown. A recent film, *Inside Out,* is a good example. It is based on the experiences of an 11-year-old girl name Riley as her family moves across the country to a new home. The larger intent is to explore human emotions. In the film, emotions such as anger and joy take the form of different characters, each struggling to control what Riley feels at any given moment. Making a film that portrays emotions is both exciting and daunting. Pixar believes that people working on such ambitious projects will eventually get lost in the creative process and be unsure about the best path forward.[24] This is particularly true in regard to their film's storyline, which evolves over time and results in many dead ends—narratives and characters that simply don't work and need to be discarded. This creates discomfort not only for the film's director but also for his or her team and even the studio at large. Large sums of money and the firm's hard-earned reputation are at stake. Directors realize that they are at risk of failing if they can't overcome the challenges they face. As noted in the introduction, a number of successful Pixar films—including *Toy Story 2*, *Ratatouille*, and *The Good Dinosaur*, were halted midproduction because they couldn't find their way. Pixar leadership did the same at Disney Animation once it took control of the studio, with the most visible example being replacing the director of the film *Brave* because of "creative differences." The directors of these films were removed from their roles (in essence, fired), and much of their existing work was discarded. Their teams were also rechartered as needed once the directors were removed. Each film team at Pixar knows that it will be given time, helpful feedback, and support as its film progresses. But it also knows what will happen if it doesn't eventually produce something that meets the high standards of the studio. This pressure, in itself, results in conflict as team members work to find the best solutions to the tests that inevitably arise in the pursuit of their goal.

N

The third task, after setting audacioius goals and accepting and even embracing the upside of conflict, is to focus the team's efforts on the areas that will make the greatest difference. In other words, not all conflict is equal. Many teams engage in a good fight, but they do so over the matters not worth fighting about. In these cases, people waste their energy on less important issues, often involving mundane operational concerns or interpersonal differences, that don't impact the group's performance. A team that engages in lower-level conflicts spends valuable time and energy on issues that distract the group from the most critical challenges it faces— the challenges that will make a difference in the success of its project or company. One reason this occurs is because higher-level conflicts are usually more difficult and threatening than lower-level conflicts. Ironically, teams under the most stress will sometimes focus on less important issues rather than the truly critical issues. I worked, for example, with a team that faced a range of threats, including the loss of market share to a new, highly agile, competitor. Instead of dealing with this challenge, members of the team wanted to talk about one individual whose behavior was disruptive but not so extreme as to warrant removing that person from the group. In essence, the team's business model was under attack, but its members wanted to talk about the interpersonal shortcomings of a fellow team member.[25] The behavior of this individual would be important if it prevented the team from addressing the key challenge it faced or was so egregious that it violated the firm's values. Instead, the focus on his behavior was simply draining attention away from more important concerns. One of the most important tasks of a team leader is to focus his or her team on the "vital few" issues and not let the group be distracted by less important issues.[26]

N

Productive conflict in teams, then, requires the following:

1. An understanding that the discomfort that comes with conflict is necessary and productive. The enemy of high performance is not conflict—it's complacency.

2. Accountability for pursuing audacious goals that generate a healthy level of tension within a team.

3. An ability to focus the team's conflict on the "vital few" areas that will make the most difference in the achievements of its goals.

4. The group having the temperament and skill needed to have a productive fight.

Fields of Conflict

TEAM MEMBERS ENGAGE IN:	Low-Quality Conflicts	High-Quality Conflicts
	"Wrong field, good plow"	"Right field, good plow"
	"Wrong field, bad plow"	"Right field, bad plow"

The next step in promoting conflict is to develop approaches that allow for a team to have a healthy debate or, more directly, a good fight.[27] How people go about fighting is second in importance only to what they fight about. The goal is to get team members to be direct in expressing their views but at the same time collaborative in being willing to take into account others' points of view and support the best solution even if it is not their idea.[28] This is meant to avoid the double-bind, where people feel they are caught in a dilemma that can't be resolved. The combination of being assertive and collaborative is difficult to achieve, but it is the sweet spot when it comes to fighting in a productive manner.

Some groups embrace techniques that encourage all team members to contribute ideas in a nonthreatening manner. In the softest form, these techniques involve some type of brainstorming (with the goal of generating more ideas than would surface in a normal team discussion). Other teams use a related technique involving "rounds," where people take turns expressing their views on a particular strategy or recommendation. Team members can't comment, other than to clarify what is being suggested, until everyone in the group has had a chance to speak. A third technique is to have everyone in the group consider before their meeting what they would recommend in regard to an important topic. They are asked to summarize their points of view in writing prior to the meeting.[29] In the meeting, each member presents his or her pre-considered view, which is then discussed as a group. This approach

generates a more robust set of alternatives and, in most cases, results in a better solution.[30] These techniques for generating ideas
are useful because everyone provides input into decisions, increasingly the likelihood that everyone will have a more or less equal
voice within a group. The best teams are those that benefit from
the collective knowledge of the group's members. A more egalitar-
ian approach stands in contrast to what occurs in many teams
where just a few people, often the team's leader or those in the
most powerful positions, dominate discussions—with other members sitting on the sidelines as observers to the team dynamic. The
techniques suggested earlier work against this tendency.

Benefiting from the team members' collective knowledge, however, requires more than generating new ideas. Debate, and conflict, is needed to test, prioritize, and improve on those ideas.
Charlan Nemeth and his team at University of California, Berkeley
examined the relative merits of brainstorming versus debate in
producing good ideas.[31] They asked people in their study to generate potential solutions to the same question, which was how to reduce traffic congestion in the San Francisco Bay area. One group
was given this question and no further guidance other than to generate as many solutions as possible. A second group was told to use
conventional brainstorming techniques, including a restriction on
judging the ideas of others. A third group was told to debate and
even challenge the ideas of others as they were presented. Brainstorming, as anticipated, resulted in more ideas being generated in
each group. But those in the study's "debate" condition, where people were encouraged to challenge each other, generated 25 percent
more ideas, on average, than those in the other two groups. The authors of this study observed, "Our findings show that debate and
criticism do not inhibit ideas but, rather, stimulate them relative to
every other condition."[32]

Pixar is notable in its ability to manage debate and criticism—
all with the intent of making films that initially "suck" (in the words
of the firm's president) into great successes. Three of the firm's
techniques are noteworthy. First, the company has daily reviews of

what individual animators have created to bring to life a small scene within the film. In particular, the animators detail the motion and features of each character. As noted in Chapter 4, during reviews called dailies, feedback and suggestions are offered in a team setting. For the animators at Pixar, conflict is part of their daily routine. Each morning, typically at 9 a.m., the film team reviews the recent shots of its animators to talk about what works and what needs to change. The feedback can be tough, to the point that some refer to it as "shredding." A second team review takes place once necessary changes are made. An observer of the process noted,

> No detail is too small to critique and no one is prohibited from arguing against the work of someone else. Everything from the angle of the lighting to the timing of certain sound effects is brought up and fought over. This intense process, sometimes called "shredding," can be draining, but the Pixar teams know that the process is vital to their ability to release quality work again and again.[33]

The primary benefit of Pixar's dailies is to help those receiving the feedback improve their work and thus the quality of the film. But the process also helps others attending the meeting who benefit from observing the group's feedback—extracting lessons that they can apply to their own work moving forward.

Pixar also has what it calls Notes, sessions where a small group of senior group leaders watches an in-progress cut of a film and offers detailed suggestions on how to make it better.[34] The focus in these sessions is primarily on the film's storyline and characters. Specific suggestions are made on how to improve the film, which is then the responsibility of the director and his or her team to assess and incorporate as they think appropriate. These suggestions surface a range of potential improvements, including what is missing from the story or what doesn't make sense. Those providing feedback need to be direct but can't simply take a film apart. People need to build on the work of others and strive to make it better. Pixar calls this plussing, a term indicating that those suggesting that something needs to change are also expected to contribute specific ideas on how to make it better. You can't simply say something is wrong—you need to suggest how to make what is wrong right. This may be impossible in some cases (if an idea or work product is fundamentally flawed), but the intent is for team members to suggest ways to improve on another's idea or work product.[35] The expectation is that every team member is responsible for pointing out when something is flawed and, just as importantly, suggesting ways to make it better. Plussing is an attempt to help the process of reviewing another's work be a positive exchange versus a series of attacks and counterattacks.

A third technique used by Pixar to surface productive conflict involves *postmortems*, which occur after a film is completed in hopes of extracting lessons learned on what went well and what needs to change in the making of the studio's next film. The postmortem after one of its films, for example, indicated that the production crew felt they were treated as being less important than the creative staff on the project. The production staff at Pixar manages a film's logistics, schedules, staffing, and money, with the goal of getting the film done on time and on budget. The perceived second-class status of the production staff occurred even though the senior leadership of the studio believed that everyone assigned to a film should be respected and invited to offer an opinion in any area of the project. The senior leadership of the studio was surprised by this finding because it was so at odds with what they believed was important and what they believed was occurring. After the postmortem, changes were made in how the groups operate to ensure that the production staff are full and valued members of the team.

✲

In teams, people need to have the emotional and social skills that minimize the downsides of conflict and, in particular, the damage that it can cause to relationships when managed poorly. The best teams are comprised of people with more effective social skills. That is, these teams have people who are better at assessing their impact on others and are able to modify their behavior as needed to manage conflict productively. Teams needs people who are tough, who can take feedback without becoming defensive, but they also need people who can give feedback and deal with conflict in a competent manner. One study, for example, examined the factors that contribute to team effectiveness. The researchers, at the Center for Collective Intelligence at MIT, found that the best small groups (defined as the groups that performed better at a number of problem-solving tasks) have several similar traits.[36] One of those traits was the ability of the team members to read the emotions of others (based on what is called a social perception test).[37] Those groups with higher levels of social sensitivity, in general, scored higher on a diverse set of problem-solving tasks. The explanation for this finding was that more-socially-skilled people are better able to work together to solve the problems they face. Their social skills result in a greater ability to tap into the knowledge and experience of each member and collectively arrive at the best solution.

Effective group decision-making centers on creating what some call psychological safety. That concept, advanced most prominently by Professor Amy Edmondson,suggests that innovative groups are better at creating an environment where people feel safe expressing who they are and what they believe.[38] In these groups, people feel that others both understand and respect their experiences, emotions, and points of view. Edmondson noted that there is "a sense of confidence that the team will not embarrass, reject or punish someone for speaking up."[39] The result is a team where it is safe for people to take risks, try new things, and ask for help. These are teams where people can admit and learn from their mistakes. Google, in a study that examined the effectiveness of hundreds of its own work teams, found psychological safety to be the single most important variable in determining a team's success.[40] The teams at Google where people feel safe are those that achieve the best results. Google is now providing its managers with training on how to foster better team results, with an emphasis on creating a necessary level of psychological safety.[41]

The point to remember, one that Edmondson reinforces in her research findings, is that psychological safety does not operate in opposition to the achievement of ambitious goals. High-performing teams set demanding goals and create a safe environment in which to pursue those goals. That said, the tendency of some is to view psychological safety as an end in itself. In extreme teams, safety always exists in combination with a strong emphasis on outcomes. This becomes particularly important when dealing with conflict. Most people intellectually understand that conflict, between individuals and within a team, can be productive. They know that growth and comfort don't always coexist. People will be uncomfortable when there is conflict, as they challenge each other in the pursuit of something significant. Yvon Chouinard, the founder of Patagonia, argues that companies need to deliberately stress themselves if they are to remain vital.[42] He believes his own firm has performed best when facing a daunting challenge or threat—even those he produced as CEO. The art of productive conflict is creating the right mix of comfort and discomfort—or, more accurately, helping people become comfortable with being uncomfortable. In these teams, people know that comfort is overrated.[43]

 **TAKEAWAYS**

> ➤ Traditional firms and teams can suffer from "terminal niceness"— creating what Jack Ma of Alibaba calls "a little white rabbit" culture.

> ➤ Cutting-edge firms and extreme teams, in contrast, realize that tension and conflict are essential to achieving their goals.

> ➤ Their skill is creating environments where people are comfortable with being uncomfortable. In so doing, they increase the likelihood that conflict is surfaced and resolved in a productive manner.

TEAMS AT THE EXTREMES

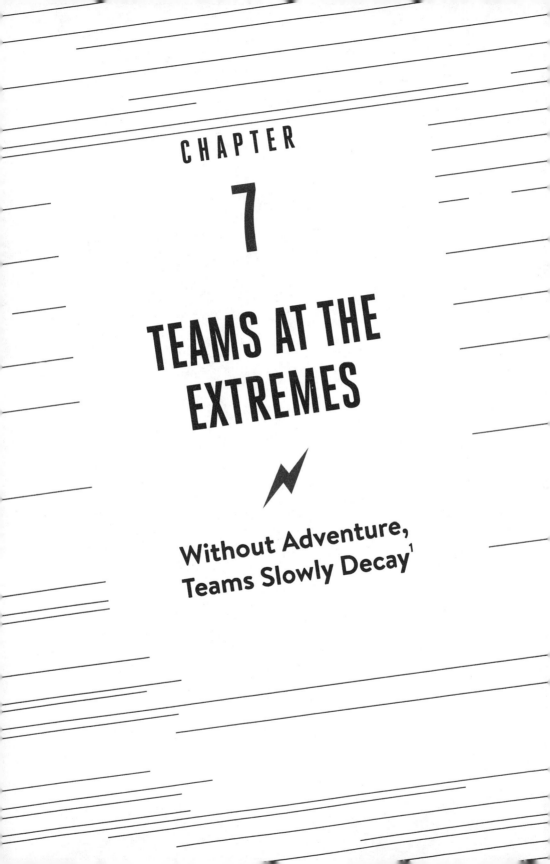

Without Adventure, Teams Slowly Decay[1]

It's no accident that the companies profiled in this book were all founded by extraordinary entrepreneurs.[2] Their businesses were built on innovative ideas that overturned the existing order of things within their industries. Netflix is disrupting the media industry through its streaming service. Airbnb is disrupting the hospitality industry through its peer-to-peer model. Alibaba is disrupting the way business is done in China through its e-commerce sites. The leaders of these firms, however, realize that their long-term success requires more than groundbreaking products and services. They need their companies, as companies, to be equally innovative—workplaces that are challenging commonly accepted ways of operating. They understand that their legacies will be based not on the products they create but on their ability to build creative and agile organizations that endure over time. Steve Jobs will always be recognized for his innovative products but the true test of his leadership will be if Apple can continue to innovate and grow for the next 50 years. Does the company he created have the people, cultures, and processes needed to do so? At this point, the jury is still out.

There is another motive that drives many of these leaders to create new types of organizations—a motive more personal and self-centered. They need to work in companies that fit their values and personalities—places they want to go to after getting up each morning and stay at when working late into the night. Brian Chesky of Airbnb describes this as entrepreneurs wanting to live in a world of their own design. They do this, at least in part, because they don't feel at home in more traditional corporations. If forced to work in a typical large company, most would either quit from frustration or be fired for insubordination. Imagine Ed Catmull of Pixar working at a studio such as Paramount. Yvon Chouinard working at L.L.Bean. John Mackey at Safeway. These scenarios seem almost absurd, which says a great deal about the idiosyncratic personalities of these leaders and how well they fit the firms they built. It also suggests the challenge that conventional firms have in attracting and retaining the talented and often quirky people they need to be successful.

Entrepreneurs, by definition, are adept at managing newness—pushing the boundaries of what exists today. The premise of this book is that cutting-edge leaders and their teams push both results and relationships further than traditional firms. But there are risks, and sometimes a price to pay, for doing so. Results, pushed too far, can produce a variety of unintended consequences, such as a harsh company culture or unethical business practices. Relationships, pushed too far, can create a soft environment that lacks the drive and toughness needed to achieve success. The paradox of building a cutting-edge firm is that an unrelenting focus on results and relationships is necessary to achieve something extraordinary but also destructive if not managed skillfully. The challenge, then, is to drive results and relationships to the breaking point while managing the very real downsides of doing so. For leaders like Reed Hastings of Netflix or Brian Chesky of Airbnb, pushing their organizations to the breaking point, pushing beyond what others believe is possible or even desirable, is not the problem. The risk they face, as does anyone who disrupts the common order of things, is that their reach exceeds their grasp.

Conventional firms face a different set of risks when it comes to results and relationships. The first is that they become all too comfortable with mediocrity. "Good enough" is the unspoken mantra in many of these groups.[3] Average results, average relationships. Often, these firms take the easy path and simply replicate strategies and practices that were successful at an earlier point in their histories.[4] Striving to profit from a firm's past successes is natural and even savvy. But the CEO of Pixar argues that many become trapped in their success and, as a result, "creatively bankrupt."[5] He believes that vital companies deliberately strive to avoid replicating what worked in the past and, instead, experiment with new approaches that challenge, or at least go beyond, what they know to be true. This, of course, doesn't mean that Pixar ignores the lessons of its past films or doesn't fully leverage the best-in-class technology and work processes that it developed over several decades of experience. But in the area of greatest importance, which in Pixar's case is telling a story that moves people, it works hard to avoid mimicking itself. Doing so is all the more difficult because organizations, in many ways, are built to standardize and reinforce what worked in the past (and, in so doing, minimize risk and maximize return). This is done through a range of mechanisms, including a group's strategies, structures, processes, and culture. Each reinforces a way of operating that developed over time and drove the growth of a firm. The result is that companies often say they want their people to be innovative but then operate in a manner that works against anything that is new and different. In so doing, they avoid the risks that come with trying that which has not been done before—but, at the same time, risk becoming tired imitations of their successful past.

A second risk facing conventional groups is disproportionately valuing either results or relationships—that is, pursuing one to the exclusion of the other. In this situation, the pursuit of results and relationships becomes an "either/or" choice.[6] Organizations and their teams believe they can focus either on results or relationships but not both at once. They do this in an attempt to simplify an overly complex world by acting as if only one side of the results/relationships dynamic truly matters. This approach fails for a number of reasons, with the most direct being the need for both to sustain a firm's performance over the long term. Results and relationships are interdependent, each needing the other, even if some believe and act otherwise. Research by John Zenger and Jo-seph Folkman underscores this point. They examined people's per-ceptions of great leadership. Two of the dimensions they probed were a leader's drive for results and the ability to build positive re-lationships. Leaders who were seen as being very strong on either results or relationships were rated by their employees as great leaders just less than 15 percent of the time.[7] In contrast, leaders who were viewed by those who work for them as being very strong on both results and relationships were rated as being great leaders 72 percent of the time. Zenger and Folkman, as you might expect, maintain that the combination of the two traits is the key to being an extraordinary leader. If we extrapolate from these findings re-garding leadership, the implication for teams is clear—great teams combine results and relationships and don't simply strive to maxi-mize one or the other.[8]

One way to portray the interplay between results and relation-ships, drawing in part on the work of Professor Amy Edmondson, is to contrast four types of teams.[9] Comfortable teams are those that value relationships over results. Stressed teams value results over relationships. Indifferent teams settle for mediocrity or worse in both areas. It is logical, then, to suggest that the best teams strive to maximize both results and relationships—to operate in the upper right quadrant of the following table. When managed well, this combination creates virtuous cycles within a team, where re-sults and relationships work in a mutually reinforcing manner to produce increasingly higher levels of performance. However, sim-ply recognizing that both are important, that they can be mutually beneficial, helps manage the tradeoffs and tensions that often exist between the two. Extreme teams take this one step further in push-ing each to the breaking point—a goal that is easy to understand but difficult to manage.[10]

Types of Teams: Results and/or Relationships

TEAM RELATIONSHIPS ARE . . .	TEAM RESULTS ARE . . .	
	Inferior	Superior
Close/Personal	*Comfortable Teams:* Members get along well but don't have the drive or toughness needed to deliver results.	*Extreme Teams:* Members work as a cohesive group to deliver extraordinary results.
Distant/Formal	*Indifferent Teams:* The team's performance is mediocre at best. Member relationships are distant or even antagonistic.	*Stressed Teams:* The team delivers results but at a cost—members feel vulnerable, isolated, and at risk.

There are two common challenges facing leaders who want to build extreme teams. The first is creating a team where no team currently exists. This may be due to the initiation of a new project or a corporate restructuring that produces new team configurations within a company. Leaders who are responsible for a new team will benefit from considering the following practices of cutting-edge firms:

Right Purpose: The need to define a compelling purpose for one's team is noted in almost every article or book on team performance. The difference in extreme teams is that they take purpose to a higher level of intensity and dedication—which is one reason they are able to attract people who are obsessed with the team's work and its reason for being. People in cutting-edge firms view their work as a calling, and the leader's responsibility is to provide them with a higher-level purpose—something beyond making money as their reason for working. The nature of a team's purpose will, of course, depend on the nature and history of the firm in which the group operates. But it should be something that authentically taps into the values and passions of the group's members—and allows them to have visible impact in those areas.

Right People: A second requirement of building a new team is hiring people who have the attributes needed for a group to be successful. But many team leaders make the mistake of focusing only on the technical or functional skills of potential hires. Extreme teams view superior capabilities as necessary but insufficient. Yes, they strive to hire smart and capable people. But they focus as much if not more on the cultural attributes that are important to their companies. A team of people who are a poor cultural fit is a problem even when the members are highly talented and motivated. The first few people hired onto a team are especially important because they set the tone for those who follow them in coming into the group. The initial hires are also responsible for building their teams and thus cast a shadow in regard to those they hire. Hiring for cultural fit in a new team means that a leader must have a clear view of the cultural attributes he or she wants and then develop an approach to effectively screen people for those attributes.

Right Priorities: Once the team's purpose and membership are set, a leader needs to clarify its vital few priorities and success metrics. In most cases, less is more when it comes to priorities and metrics. These imperatives should be few in number and clearly communicated across a group or team, with everyone knowing the goal and the plan of how to achieve it.[11] This includes an explanation of the larger context in which the team operates and how the group will address specific opportunities and challenges in that environment. Airbnb is an example of a firm that is rigorous in clarifying what needs to be done each year to move the company forward. The firm's annual goals are summarized on a single page of paper (The Sheet), which is communicated throughout the organization. Once a firm's goals are clearly articulated, teams then set their own goals and responsibilities. An important element of setting priorities is determining how accountability will be assigned. Teams vary in how they do this, with some looking to individuals within a group to take the lead on a particular initiative (but working with other team members as needed to achieve the group's goals). Other teams prefer that the team members in total take responsibility for the group's goals, in order to create a greater sense of shared ownership. Each of these approaches can work, but the essential point is to clarify the team's priorities, success measures, and accountabilities combined with local autonomy to determine how to best execute those priorities.

Right Practices: Leaders of new teams need to determine the desired culture of their teams. At the simplest level, this means identifying the few essential beliefs and behaviors that will define what is expected of group members. Some describe this as clarifying what team members must always do and what they must never do. Then, the leader, often with the members of the team, define the work and management practices that reinforce the desired cultural attributes. Netflix, for example, believes in a "freedom and responsibility" culture and has created a range of organizational practices that fully and consistently support it (such as placing no restrictions on vacation time because it views people as adults who are able to determine when and how much vacation time they need). The other lesson from extreme teams is that culture is most productively viewed through the lens of what people experience while working in a group. Airbnb, for example, looks at a wide range of factors that influence employee experiences, with a focus on creating a sense of community and belonging. This starts with the work itself and giving people a great deal of say in the projects of interest to them, as well as the management of their day-to-day work. But it also involves a wide range of company practices that impact how employees experience the company, such as the design of the corporate office or the ability to work remotely when needed. These factors at Airbnb are managed primarily at a company level, but the concept of focusing on and enhancing member experience holds true for teams as well.

Start-Up Questions for the Leaders of New Teams

→ What higher-level purpose will guide and motivate your new team members? Can you express this purpose in a succinct and impactful manner?

→ What are the values and traits that you need in team members to achieve your purpose? What process will you use to screen people for these attributes?

→ What are the vital few priorities and metrics that will define your team's success? How will you ensure that all team members understand the reasons behind these priorities and how they are related to their goals?

→ What team work practices will you use to support the team's work and ensure progress on the priorities? What are the value-added topics for the team's meetings and how should they be managed?

→ What culture do you want within the team and the experience of working within it? What practices and norms will you use to reinforce the culture?

→ How will you ensure that key issues are surfaced within the team and conflicts are managed effectively?

New teams have the advantage of a clean slate and can design how they will operate without the burdens of the past. In particular, they can benefit from the innovative practices of other firms to develop approaches that fit their specific needs. The eyeglass firm Warby Parker is such an example. It is a mission-driven business that operates with a "buy a pair, give a pair" business model. Each time a customer buys a pair of the firm's glasses, a second pair is donated to someone in a developing country. The company, from its founding, benchmarked other cutting-edge firms and incorporated the ideas it found most useful. For example, Warby Parker, like Zappos, wants to hire people whose beliefs and style match its cultural principles. It believes that technical skill doesn't mean that someone can get things done with the firm, particularly in regard to gaining the support of others on one's team. The firm has a set of cultural principles, such as "Set ambitious goals and measure results" and "Inject fun and quirkiness into everything we do." It screens potential hires by asking for behavioral examples that assess each principle (in regard to quirkiness, it will ask, "What was the last costume you wore?" or "What do you like to do for fun?"). Warby Parker, like Patagonia, also strives to create a work environment designed to support its employees, including cross-group learning programs and a flexible work policy. A third example of taking what other firms have done is the use of ongoing peer feedback, similar to what is found at Netflix. At Warby Parker, this means that everyone in the company receives 360-degree feedback each quarter. The goal at Warby Parker is not to mimic others but to understand what is possible as it developed a culture that fit its unique personality.

/

An even more frequent and difficult challenge is turning around a stagnant or failing team. This need becomes particularly salient when a new leader, often with no history with a group, is tasked with its revitalization. The need to turn around a team also surfaces when a long-tenured leader feels that he or she is investing an inordinate amount of time and energy to get a team to perform at a high level or when a business has grown to a point that outpaces the ability of the current teams to meet the challenges ahead. The first step in revitalizing a stagnant team is to assess as objectively as possible the group's performance. The leader knows that his or her team is underperforming, but the specifics need to be examined. There are two key questions to answer at this point in the turnaround process:

→ Does the team deliver results consistent with what is expected by its organization, leaders, and customers?

→ Does the team foster productive working relationships among its members as well as with those in other groups?

The measures of a team's performance vary by team but often include both outcome measures (such as sales and revenue) and process measures (such as milestone achievements and budget performance). As noted earlier, however, the key is to look at metrics that are closely linked to the firm's purpose. Pixar, for example, tracks a film's progress against myriad hard measures, but it also assesses the creative depth of its storyline—which is harder to measure but even more essential to the success of a team. These metrics should be augmented by more informal input from a team's customers, as well as its members. These perceptions may not always be on the mark but should be considered in the leader's assessment of the group. The other factor to consider is the quality of the relationships among the members of the team. The leader will want to determine, through observations and interviews, how people are working together as a group and partnering with other groups within their organization. Pixar, for instance, views the quality of team member relationships as a key indicator in determining a team's health and ability to eventually deliver an extraordinary film. Teams where people do not "gel," where there is a low level of energy and trust, are seen as broken in the Pixar culture.

The next task is to identify the causes of the team's poor performance, particularly in relation to the performance gaps uncovered in the above assessment. This root cause analysis is intended to identify the factors, often unrecognized, that are hindering the group's performance. A leader needs to be leery of assuming that he or she knows what is causing the team to perform below expectations. That is, many leaders jump to the wrong conclusions in seeking to quickly identify what ails their groups. The leader may have a theory of what is wrong but can't assume that it is the only or even the most important area that needs to change. In particular, a leader needs to beware of mistaking symptoms for causes. For example, he or she may assume that the people within the team lack motivation and drive (and, as a result, determine that changes are needed in the team's composition). However, the deeper issue is that team members are getting unclear and even conflicting direction from the senior leadership within the firm. They have learned that being passive is the best option for them because the direction from those above them shifts on a regular basis. Leaders seeking to understand their underperforming teams need to look for the deeper issues that influence other, often more noticeable, behaviors or outcomes.

One of the most productive ways of uncovering the drivers of underperformance is to probe the differences between what people espouse as being important and how they act.[12] Every group has times when what it says is different from what it does—but these contradictions are typically more pronounced in a dysfunctional team. For instance, the animators at Disney at the time of the Pixar acquisition were highly talented and passionate about their craft. Yet their studio was turning out unimaginative films that were failing creatively (as well as commercially). The question, then, was, "Why do talented and committed people continue to produce films at odds with what they say is important?" A new leader will want to look for the most salient contradictions within a team and then pull them apart to see what they reveal. In many cases, the truths uncovered are those that people within a company or team don't fully recognize or don't want to face. The key, for those leading a turnaround, is to recognize the value of contradictions in understanding what is going on within a team—paying particular attention to aspects of the team that are surprising or puzzling. The goal, then, is to surface the group's contradictions, understand why they exist, and analyze their impact on the group's results.[13]

Teams, of course, also fail due to a variety of self-inflicted wounds.[14] Some teams, for example, are unclear as to their purpose or have a purpose that is so mundane that it fails to motivate its members. Other teams don't have the people needed to be successful. I find in my work that leaders often overestimate the quality of the talent on their teams and their ability to meet the challenges they face. Consider a team that is responsible for the sales of its firm's products in markets outside the United States. The team is comprised, however, of people with no international experience, with all of the members having lived and worked only in the United States. This lack of experience will most likely result in a faulty understanding of how markets outside the United States operate and, as a result, poor decisions on how to best compete in those markets. A related type of failure occurs when a team is comprised of people who were successful in the past but lack the skills needed to be successful in the future, given the challenges and opportunities the team will face. A marketing team, for example, that was successful for years before the explosion of social media may lack the expertise needed to take advantage of the new technologies. In this situation, the talent on the team lags due to changes in technology and the marketplace—changes that require new ways of thinking and a new sets of skills.

Another common trait of failing teams is a lack of clarity regarding priorities. Failing teams are often distracted and pulled away from the critical few priorities that will determine their success. Often, these teams try to accomplish too many priorities or fail to sequence their priorities in an effective manner. Instead, they become distracted by more mundane or administrative concerns that take time and energy away from the truly important areas that require their attention. A related mistake occurs when the team focuses on the right priorities but defines them in such a vague manner that its people are unclear about what success looks like or what needs to be done to achieve success. The leader of a new team will also want to examine the group's work practices. Failing groups often take too long to make decisions or make them in a flawed manner (for example, by not considering relevant data, failing to explore a necessary range of options, or allowing a few members to dominate group discussions and solutions). These groups, in particular, are less capable of surfacing and managing conflict. Some teams dislike contentious exchanges among team members and avoid discussions in which their members hold conflicting views. The "off limits" topics within a team can involve the most important issues that it needs to address (such as a strategy to address an emerging competitor or the reasons a key initiative is failing).

A final area to assess is the practices of the team and how they impact its culture. This is one of the most challenging aspects of a team's turnaround because existing cultures are notoriously difficult to change. Many leaders know what they want in regard to culture but have no formal plan to make that desired state come about. To say, for example, that you want people to be more comfortable with conflict will have little impact unless specific actions are taken to make that intent a reality (for example, training people on their conflict management styles, developing robust practices to surface divergent points of view within a group, rewarding those who are skillful in surfacing and managing conflict, or providing feedback to those who avoid conflict or settle for easy compromises). The leader of a team turnaround effort needs to be bold in changing the mindset and behavior of his or her group. For instance, he or she may promote onto the team more junior members who have the traits that the leader wants to see in the other members of the team. These individuals may, for example, possess an entrepreneurial mindset that is needed if the team is to be successful. Or a new team member may be more willing than others to challenge the leader and other team members when needed to move the group and business forward. In so doing, the new members are modeling a more open style that the leader wants to see from all of the team members.

⚡

Starting a new team and turning around a stagnant team are challenges that most leaders will face at some point during their careers. Both situations underscore the importance to a leader of getting his or her team right in order to produce results. But few ideas in business are as embraced, and then undermined, as teamwork.[15] Organizations and their leaders value what teams can achieve and are quick to talk about the benefits of collaboration. But many fail to provide the support that teams need to be successful. In some cases, this is due to a lack of understanding of what teams must have to be successful (such as the right purpose or right people). That said, the leaders of the firms in this book are notable in that they didn't start out with deep knowledge of the psychology and sociology of team behavior. They knew what they wanted (and didn't want) in their culture and teams, trusted their instincts in trying new things, and, to paraphrase John Mackey of Whole Foods, were willing to make it up as they went along.

The problem, in most cases, is not a lack of knowledge but an unwillingness to give up control. As firms grow, they necessarily develop processes to standardize and monitor their increasingly complex organizations. Coordinating the efforts of thousands of people, often spread across multiple groups and geographies, is no easy task. The answer, in many cases, is to develop formal mechanisms intended to control what occurs within the company. This response becomes even more likely when a group experiences mistakes or threats of various types, as leadership attempts to get things back on track and prevent future problems. Airbnb, for instance, initially had no real process to handle safety issues when they arose in one of its rental units. If you are a host, you want Airbnb to have the best process possible to deal with problems you encounter. Airbnb is not unique. Patagonia had no real process to train its new managers in how to manage a store team. Pixar had no real process to ensure that its employees did not work to the point of creating repetitive stress injuries. Processes, in the right form, are necessary and helpful to customers, employees, and companies.[16] The problem is that good intentions can produce a negative outcome. Processes spread and, in the aggregate, can result in a stifling bureaucracy that is resistant to change. In short, organizations create processes that, by definition, are "hardwired" and not adaptive to changing conditions.

Companies that want the benefits of extreme teams need to give them autonomy to do what they believe is needed given the challenges they face. If process limits what they can do, the upside of having a team is also limited. That said, giving teams autonomy is not without risk, as a strong team will inevitably challenge the formal and informal control systems within a company. The result is that many organizations say they want strong teams, but in fact, they don't. They want effective but compliant teams that don't threaten the status quo, including existing company practices and processes. This is not to suggest that teams should be allowed to do whatever they want regardless of the consequences. Or that a firm should do away with hierarchical controls and necessary processes. The reality is that strong teams, even those that are successful, can create problems for a company.

Teams can also be a problem in being perceived as threats to their own leaders. Team dynamics always have some element of power underlying how they operate. Much is written about how power can inhibit people on a team from expressing their points of view because they fear alienating the team's leader or other powerful group members. But equally important, and less discussed, is the ability of teams to threaten a leader's security in regard to power. The reality is that some leaders view their teams with a degree of ambivalence.[17] Teams can quit on a leader. Teams can provide negative feedback about a leader to those in more senior positions. They can also compete with the leader, with some members thinking they should be leading the group. Some leaders, seeking to protect themselves, will go as far as to

undermine their own teams in an attempt to limit what they per-
ceive to be threats. People who have worked in corporations for
any length of time see peer groups competing or even undermining each other in the pursuit of power. Some will subvert other
groups if such actions enhance their own standing with a company. But the point I am making here goes one step further, suggesting that leaders at times will undermine their own teams if it
enhances their own positions within their companies. In particular, the most talented member of a team can be viewed as a
threat to the leader if other team members are more inclined to
follow that individual or even believe that current leader should
be replaced by another within the group. The willingness of a
leader to undermine his or her team is counterintuitive because a
failing team is certainly career limiting for power-hungry individuals. But consider that some leaders want to avoid failure yet at
the same keep control over their positions of power. Which becomes preeminent depends on the leader and the situation.

A recent study by social psychologists Charleen Chase and Jon
Maner suggests how this can happen.[18] The researchers first assessed their study's participants on their power motivation using a
survey designed to identify those for whom power is very important. They then placed the study participants into different experi-
mental conditions in which they were led to believe that their
power was either secure or potentially at risk. The researchers gave
the participants a task in which they needed to create high-performing teams by assigning people to particular groups based on
their skills and ability to work together—with the prospect of rewards for the teams that performed well. The research findings indicate that "power hungry" leaders whose positions of power are
unsure will at times sabotage their own teams and, in particular,
the most talented individuals within those teams to preserve their
personal power. In one study, for example, leaders with a high
power motive, when given the choice, separated the most talented
individual in a group from others on the team (by having that individual work alone on a task). In another, they were more likely to

limit the degree to which their team members could communicate with each other. These leaders did this even knowing that having team members interact and cooperate would improve their group's results. One of the study's authors noted, "It's surprising to me just how willing leaders are to really undermine group success in favor of their own power."[19] This is not to suggest that all leaders act in such a Machiavellian manner—those without a dominant power motive in these studies did not demonstrate the destructive behavior noted here. In addition, the behavior was not evident when a leader believed his or her power base was secure. But the reality of corporate life is that people with a need for power often move up in a company and battle to gain or sustain their positions—and as a result, they will in some cases put protecting their own authority above the success of their teams.

✎

Teams are seductive because they offer a clear advantage when designed and managed well—an advantage that is difficult for others to copy. But extraordinary teams are less common than we would think because they come with a steep price—notably the need for organizations and their leaders to give up control. Many organizations and leaders don't want to take the risk of trying things that have not been done before. Many don't want the angst and uncertainty that comes with giving teams the freedom to operate as they see fit. In turn, some team members don't want the responsibility that comes with being given that power. They may say they want it but then realize the burden of being fully accountable that comes with it. We thus find people at all levels in a company who collectively support the idea of teams—but lack the commitment and creativity to make them work.[20]

Almost all great achievements, in business and society, are the result of small groups of people working together to achieve ambitious goals.[21] The leaders of these groups select who becomes members of their teams and then motivate them to achieve more than they thought possible. These leaders deserve the accolades that come their way when their teams perform well. It is the team, however, that delivers on the leader's vision even though its members are typically unknown outside of the organization in which they work. Teams, not individuals, make the difference. The best teams provide another, equally important, benefit. They meet the need of most people to work with others to achieve something greater than themselves. This is evident in a story involving the father of a friend of mine. He fought in World War II as part of a bomber crew that flew missions over Germany to defeat the Nazis. I went to visit him many years later when he was in his 90s. As we sat talking, I noticed on the wall an aged black and white photograph of a group of young men standing in front of a plane. These were the men he served with over seventy years ago. All of the other crew members, ten in number, were dead as a result of the war or from old age. I asked about the photograph and my friend's father said to me, "I look at it every day and say out loud the name of each crew member." I don't tell this story to glorify war or to suggest that working in a corporate team is the equivalent of going into battle with one's life on the line. I am, however, suggesting that there is a deep human need to bond with others, often in a risky endeavor, in the pursuit of a larger or even heroic purpose. Extreme teams provide that opportunity.

ACKNOWLEDGMENTS

Many have studied teams seeking to explain why some work well while others fail. One of the most notable is J. Richard Hackman, who spent nearly five decades observing and writing about teams. Richard was my advisor in graduate school and proved to be a wise and quirky mentor. Dennis N.T. Perkins, author of *Leading at the Edge*, was an inspiration in emphasizing the importance of entrepreneurial leadership in building great teams and organizations. Robert Freed Bales, in his pioneering work on group dynamics, examined what he called task-oriented versus socioemotional behavior in team life. His ideas influenced what I describe in this book as the interplay between results and relationships. Other individuals who provided helpful insights, either in person or through their writing, include David Berg in *Paradoxes of Group Life*, Amy Edmondson in *Teaming,* Jon Katzenbach in *The Wisdom on Teams*, David Nadler in *Executive Teams*, and Ruth Wageman in *Senior Leadership Teams.* Barry Johnson was generous in discussing with me his insights into how polarities influence what occurs in organizations and teams. I especially want to thank the many clients and colleagues with whom I worked as a consultant on the building of high-performing organizations. They gave me hands-on experience working closely with teams and leaders doing important work. I also benefited by working with Stephen S. Power and his group of professionals at AMACOM. Stephen offered editorial advice throughout the writing this book. Finally, I am grateful for the support provided by my daughter Gabrielle and brother John.

CHAPTER NOTES

Introduction – Revolutionizing the Way We Work

1 *Fortune* magazine's annual ratings of best places to work (100 Best Places to Work). Whole Foods has made the top 100 ranking every year since the rating came out (1998) and is the top job creator among those making the ratings over those years.

2 Whole Foods does not use the term *employees*—those who work for the firm are called *team members*. Outsiders may view this as semantics, but the difference is important to Whole Foods. I do, however, use the term employee in this book for the sake of clarity in some instances.

3 Whole Foods has recently increased the degree to which it orders products centrally in order to compete more aggressively on price with a host of emerging competitors. But the firm's basic model of store and team autonomy remains intact.

4 See Charles Fishman, "The Anarchist's Cookbook," *Fast Company*, July 2004.

5 See Charles Fishman, "Whole Foods Is All Teams," *Fast Company*, Issue 2 April/May 1996. A manager at Whole Foods noted, "If there's someone who's not working hard, who's not putting in everything they can, the team can say, 'You know what? We don't want you to drag us down.'" Abha Bhattarai, "At Whole Foods, a 'Survivor'-Like Ritual," *The Washington Post*, June 24, 2012.

6 Matthew Sturdevant, "Whole Teamwork Is a Natural," *Hartford Courant*, September 21, 2014. Whole Foods, of course, is not a perfect company, and it attracts critics for a number of reasons, including what some see as its premium pricing. But one thing is certain about Whole Foods—it will never be confused with Safeway.

7 John Mackey and Rajendra Sisodia, *Conscious Capitalism: Liberating the Heroic Spirit of Business*, Harvard Business Review Press, 2014, 91.

8 Fishman, "The Anarchist's Cookbook."

9 See Fishman, "Whole Foods Is All Teams."

10 These Whole Foods inspections are called TCS reviews ("The Customer Snapshot").

11 See Fishman, "Whole Foods Is All Teams."

12 Nick Paumgarten, "Food Fighter: Does Whole Foods' C.E.O. Know What's Best for You?" *New Yorker*, January 4, 2010.

13   Rob Cross, Reb Rebele, and Adam Grant, "Collaborative Overload," January-February 2016.

14   See J. R. Hackman, *Why Team's Don't Work: Theory and Research on Small Groups,* ed. R. Scott Tindal et al. (New York: Plenum Press, 1998). Richard provides a thorough list of what can go wrong with teams.

15   See J. R. Hackman, *Leading Teams* (Harvard Business Review Press, 2002)

16   See Steven J. Karau and Kipling D Williams, "Social Loafing: A Meta-Analytic Review and Theoretical Integration," *Journal of Personality and Social Psychology* 65 (1993): 681–706.

17   Pixar now has an ergonomist who comes into the studio on a regular basis to adjust the workstations of animators who spend long hours on the computers.

18   Pixar cofounder Ed Catmull interview with Travis Smiley on PBS: "There's a cultural ethic, which is that we're making films that touch the world. That's what we want to do, touch them emotionally. For me, there's something grand about that view of the world." www.pbs.org/wnet/ tavissmiley/interviews/pixar-co-founder-ed-catmull-2/#

19   Ed Catmull notes in *Creativity Inc.* (New York: Random House, 2014), "The takeaway here is worth repeating: Getting the team right is the necessary precursor to getting the ideas right. It is easy to say you want talented people, and you do, but the way those people interact with one another is the real key. Even the smartest people can form an ineffective team if they are mismatched. That means it is better to focus on how a team is performing, not on the talents of the individuals within it. A good team is made up of people who complement each other."

20   Interview with Robert Bruce Shaw.

21   Pixar's CEO notes, "We will support the leader for as long and as hard as we can, but the thing we cannot overcome is if they have lost the crew. It's when the crew says we are not following that person. We say we are 'director led,' which implies they make all the final decisions. What it means to us is the director has to lead and the way we can tell when they are not leading is if people say 'we are not following.'" Ed Catmull interview, Economist Innovation Summit, March 2010, www.economist. com/events-conferences/americas/innovation-2010?bclid=60841074800 1&bctid=596049420001.

22   Anthony Lane, "The Fun Factory: Life at Pixar," *New Yorker*, May 16, 2011.

23   Interview with Robert Bruce Shaw.

24   M. S. Clark and J. Mills. "The Difference Between Communal and Exchange Relationships: What it Is and Is Not." *Personality and Social Psychology Bulletin* 19 (1993): 684–91.

25   Keith Wrightson, *English Society: 1580–1680* (New Brunswick: Rutgers University Press, 2003).

26   Patagonia's founder, Yvon Chouinard, wrote of his firm's child care center: "A family-friendly business tries to blur that distinction between work and family and work and play. For us, a quality workplace includes one of the best child care centers anywhere. The law requires that there be no more than four infants for every caregiver. At our center we have only three infants per caregiver. The law also states that there be no more than 12 two-year-olds per caregiver. At our center there are no more than five." (Presented at the Conference on Corporate Citizenship, Georgetown University, Washington, D.C., May 16, 1996, clinton6.nara. gov/1996/05/1996-05-16-white-house-conference-on-corporate-citizenship.html.)

27   Pankaj Aggarwal, "The Effects of Brand Relationship Norms on Consumer Attitudes and Behavior," *Journal of Consumer Research* 31 (2004), 87–101. Also of interest: Josh Barro, "Sorry, but Your Favorite Company Can't Be Your Friend," *New York Times*, December 11, 2015.

28   Disney acquired Pixar in 2006. However, Pixar's leaders were put in charge of Disney Animation (a reverse takeover of sorts).

29   Amazon, one of those early competitors, acquired Zappos in 2009.

30   Note: All figures are from public sources for 2015 unless noted. The mottos listed are in some cases my interpretation of public statements made by a firm or its leaders (which I used when a recognized motto was absent from the company's literature).

31   See Pixar's LinkedIn page (www.linkedin.com/company/pixar-animation-studios), which reads: "Pixar's objective is to combine proprietary technology and world-class creative talent to develop computer-animated feature films with memorable characters and heartwarming stories that appeal to audiences of all ages."

32   This is the worldwide box office as reported from two films—*Inside Out* and *The Good Dinosaur*. Note that Pixar does not always release two films each year, and in the past, one film every year or two was the norm. Annual revenue for Pixar is not available; it is included in the Walt Disney Company's total revenue from all of its studios (which was $7.36 billion in 2015).

33   Netflix has tried a number of mission statements/mottos, but none have staying power. The first two listed here are from statements by the firm's CEO, and the last is from the Netflix company webpage in regard to its competition (ir.netflix.com/long-term-view.cfm). In a recent interview, the firm's CEO joked that his vision was to make the world less productive

34   Patagonia company webpage, www.patagonia.com/us/patagonia.go?assetid=2047.

35   See Alibaba Group company webpage:www.alibabagroup.com/en/about/overview

36   Leo Tolstoy, *Anna Karenina* (New York: Penguin Classics, 2004). Peter Thiel, a venture capitalist, appears to suggest the reverse in saying that successful start-up firms are all different in offering something unique while unsuccessful start-ups are all alike in offering similar products and services. His focus, however, is on a firm's competitive offering and not how it operates in regard to its internal practices and culture (which is my focus).

37   This is not to suggest that high-performing teams are monolithic—there are real differences but they also share a common set of core attributes (such as embracing a few carefully selected team norms regarding member behavior). See Richard Hackman, "Why Teams Don't Work," *Harvard Business Review* May (2009). Another well-regarded book on teams

is Douglas Smith and Jon Katzenbach, *The Wisdom of Teams: Creating the High-Performance* (Boston: Harvard Business Review Press, 2015).

38   See Tara C. Reich and M. Sandy Hershcovis, "Interpersonal Relationships at Work," in APA Handbook of Industrial and Organizational Psychology, ed. S. Zedek et al. (Washington, D.C.: American Psychological Association, 2011), 241.

39   For an in-depth analysis of why firms and their teams avoid conflict, see Richard Pascal, *Surfing the Edge of Chaos: The Laws of Nature and the New Laws of Business.* (New York: Crown Business, 2001).

40   Zappos Insights website, "Our Unique Culture: Build a Positive Team and Family Spirit," www.zapposinsights.com/about/zappos/our-unique-culture.

41   Zappos notes on its webpage, "We are more than just a team though—we are a family. We watch out for each other, care for each other, and go above and beyond for each other because we believe in each other and we trust each other. We work together, but we also play together. Our bonds go far beyond the typical 'co-worker' relationships found at most other companies."

42   Most of these firms also have critics who find fault with their business model or practices. Airbnb, for example, is found wanting by some who believe it operates in a manner that crowds out low-cost housing in urban areas by turning units into a new form of hotels. Alibaba is criticized by some for its acceptance of the Chinese government's restrictions on internet traffic. Whole Foods is chastised by some for working hard to keep unions out of their stores. Each of the firms profiled in this book aspires to a higher purpose but few are free of controversy.

Chapter 1: Results and Relationships

1   T. S. Elliott wrote: "Only those who will risk going too far can possibly find out how far one can go." Preface to Harry Crosby, *Transit of Venus* (1931), p. ix.

2   The initial business plan for Netflix was to sell movies on DVDs, but the firm quickly switched to rentals.

3   Gina Keating, "Five Myths about Netflix," *The Washington Post*, February 21, 2014.

4   Gina Keating, "Netflixed: The Epic Battle for America's Eyeballs," *Portfolio*, 2013.

5   In 2000, Blockbuster had $5 billion in revenue while Netflix had $10 million.

6   Netflix was founded in 1997. Blockbuster filed for bankruptcy on September 23, 2010. Bought by Viacom in 1994 for $8.4 billion, Blockbuster was worth only $24 million at the time of the bankruptcy filing.

7   The massive size of Netflix is reflected in how it dominates Internet use. See Neil Hughes, "Netflix Boasts 37% Share of Internet Traffic in North

America, Compared with 3% for Apple's iTunes," *Apple Insider*, January 20, 2016.

8   "Netflix Culture: Freedom and Responsibility." Internal presentation, available at www.slideshare.net/reed2001/culture-1798664.

9   Nancy Hass, "And the Award for the Next HBO Goes To . . . ," *GQ*, January 29, 2013.

10   Hastings also believes that putting his firm's principles in writing promotes productive debate within the company (such as the degree to which the principles are being followed) and how to most clearly communicate them (clarifying statements that may be confusing).

11   From Greylock Partners, "Blitzscaling 16: Reed Hastings on Building a Steaming Empire," www.youtube.comwatch?v=jYhP08uuffs&sns=em.

12   Netflix blog post announcing the unlimited maternity and paternity leave policy, blog.netflix.com/2015/08/starting-now-at-netflix-unlimited. html.

13   La Verdad, December 27, 2010 (1:06 p.m.), posted on "Hacking Netflix," www.hackingnetflix.com/2010/12/whats-it-really-like-to-work-at-netflix.html.

14   Comment posted by former Netflix vice president on the website *Glassdoor*. Regarding Netflix, it reads, "A bit of a culture of fear articulated as 'the sniper in the building,' as some new hires and long-time employees are either bad fits or fail to grow, and are subsequently let go. Culture emphasizes experimentation, which includes needed organizational experiments, and this type of experimentation also reinforces the fear. Again, most of this well-articulated in culture deck, so no surprise." www. glassdoor.com/Reviews/Employee-Review-Netflix-RVW2115622.htm.

15   Patty McCord, "How Netflix Reinvented HR," *Harvard Business Review* January-February (2014).

16   Robert J. Grossman, "Tough Love at Netflix," SHRM 55 (2010).

17   "Netflix Culture: Freedom and Responsibility."

18   The firm's CEO, Reed Hastings, said the company let go of approximately 1,000 people over its history without a single lawsuit. Interview with *Blitzscaling* 16: Reed Hastings on Building a Streaming Empire. https:// www.youtube.com/watch?v=jYhP08uuffs. Nov. 12, 2015.

19   Grossman, "Tough Love at Netflix."

20   Jodi Kantor and David Streitfeld, "Inside Amazon: Wrestling Big Ideas in a Bruising Workplace," *New York Times*, August 15, 2015.

21   The *New York Times* is a competitor of the *Washington Post*, which was acquired by Jeff Bezos several years ago. Some of those supporting Amazon suggest that the *Times* article is biased as a result.

22   John Cook, "Facebook, Amazon Staffers Are the Most Stressed: Google, Microsoft Are the Best Paid," *Geekwire*, June 6, 2001.

23   Amazon is not alone in this practice as other firms, such as Walmart, use similar technologies to eliminate what some refer to as "time theft."

24   Joe Nocera, "Jeff Bezos and the Amazon Way," *New York Times*, August 21, 2015.

25   Amazon corporate site, "Our Leadership Principles," www.amazon.jobs/ principles.

26   Spencer Soper, "Amazon Warehouse Workers Complain of Harsh Conditions," *Los Angeles Times*, October 1, 2011.

27   The *Times* did not indicate how often this occurs, but Amazon, in responding to the article, suggested that the large majority of the comments in its feedback process are positive (by a ratio of five positive comments to every one negative comment).

28   Amazon grew from $6.92B in revenue in 2004 to $88.99 billion in 2014.

29   Those who invested $1,000 in Amazon at the time of its public offering now have stock worth over $350,000, based on an initial IPO price of $18 in 1997 and a price of $531 in 2015 (post stock splits).This stock as of September 2016 is trading even higher, approaching $800 per share.

30   Jeff Bezos in Amazon's 1997 shareholder letter, media.corporate-ir.net/media_files/irol/97/97664/reports/Shareholderletter97.pdf.

31   Brad Stone, *The Everything Store: Jeff Bezos and the Age of Amazon* (New York: Little, Brown and Company, 2013), 131.

32   There are various definitions of what constitutes a team and also various types of teams. Susan Cohen, a team's researcher, suggests the following as the most general definition: "Team is a collection of individuals who are interdependent in the their tasks, who share responsibility for outcomes, who see themselves and are seen by others an intact social entity embed in one or more larger social systems and who manage their relationships across organizational boundaries." "See What Makes a Team Work," *Journal of Management* 23 (1997), 241.

33   J. Richard Hackman outlines three criteria to assess a team's effectiveness: 1) The team's output is acceptable to its clients, 2) The team's capabilities improve over time, and 3) Working in the team is satisfying to its members. See Hackman, *Leading Teams: Setting the Stage for Great Performances* (Boston: Harvard Business Press, 2002), 30.

34   Amanda Little, "An Interview with Patagonia Founder Yvon Chouinard," *Grist*, October 23, 2004.

35   Megan Hustad, "Whole Foods' John Mackey: Self-Awareness on Aisle 5?" *Fortune*, March 8, 2013.

36   Ian Parker, "How an Industrial Designer Became Apple's Greatest Product," February 23, 2015.

37   Jay Yarow, "Jony Ive: This Is the Most Important Thing I Learned from Steve Jobs," *Business Insider*, October 10, 2014.

38   Robert Putnam, *Bowling Alone: The Collapse and Revival of American Community* (New York: Simon & Schuster, 2001).

39   There is a great deal of research on the impact of social cohesion on performance. See D. J. Beal et al., "Cohesion and Performance in Groups: A Meta-Analytic Clarification of Construct Relation," *Journal of Applied Psychology* 88 (2003), 989–1004; S. M. Gully, D. J. Devine, and D. J. Whitney, "A Meta-Analysis of Cohesion and Performance: Effects of Level of Analysis and Task Interdependence," *Small Group Research* 26 (1995): 497–520; M. A. Hogg, *The Social Psychology of Group Cohesiveness* (New York: New York University Press, 1993).

40   Dora L. Costa and Matthew E. Kahn, *Heroes and Cowards: The Social Forces of War* (Princeton: Princeton University Press, 2008).

41 An important caveat: The authors found the camaraderie exerted this level of influence only when the soldiers saw others in their troop as similar to themselves—in their place of birth, ethnicity, social standing, and age. See Costa and Kahn, *Heroes and Cowards: The Social Forces of War.*

42 "Item 10: I Have a Best Friend at Work," *Gallup*, www.gallup.com/businessjournal/511/item-10-best-friend-work.aspx.

43 Some observers of culture make a distinction between cognitive culture and emotional culture. Cognitive culture includes shared intellectual values, norms, and assumptions. Emotional culture involves the feelings people have in regard to these values, norms, and assumptions. See "Manage Your Emotional Culture." Sigal Barsade and Olivia A. O'Neill. *Harvard Business Review*, January-February (2016).

44 The academic literature examines this topic under the banner of social cohesion. An expansive definition of cohesion reads, "The strength of the bonds linking individuals to the group, the unity of the group, feelings of attraction for specific group members and the group itself, the unity of the group and the degree to which group members coordinate their efforts to achieve goals." iChapters, Thomson Learning, 2006, 14. See also John Bruhn, *The Group Effect: Social Cohesion and Health Outcomes* (New York: Springer, 2009).

45 Christopher Rhoads and Li Yuan, "How Motorola Fell a Giant Step Behind: As It Milked Thin Phone, Rivals Sneaked Ahead on the Next Generation," *Wall Street Journal*, April 27, 2007.

46 For an analysis of the physical, emotional, and social impact of isolation, see John T. Cacioppo and William Patrick, *Loneliness: Human Nature and the Need for Social Connection* (New York: Norton, 2009).

47 Susan T. Fiske, Amy J. C. Cuddy, and Petter Glick, "Universal Dimension of Social Cognition: Warmth and Competence," *Trends in Cognitive Science* 11 (2006): 77–79.

48 Teresa Amabile, Colin M. Fisher, and Julianna Pillemer, "IDEO's Culture of Helping," *Harvard Business Review*, January-February (2015).

49 There is a long history of group research that looks at the dynamic between results and relationships in small groups. Different terms are used, but the general idea that teams must manage both weaves through the literature. The early work in this area was done at Harvard by Robert Feed Bales. See his book *Social Interaction Systems: Theory and Measurement* (London: Transaction Publishers, 2001). Later work focuses on the concept of group cohesion and how it impacts performance, as noted above.

50 Google bought Fadell's firm for $3.2 billion in 2014. Fadell departed Google in 2016.

51 See Connie Loizos, "Is Tony Fadell in Nest's Way?" *Techcrunch*, March 30, 2016. Also see Lydia Dishman, "What's Going on at Nest?" *Fast Company*, February 17, 2016.

52 Steve Lohr, "Tony Fadell Steps Down Amid Tumult at Nest, a Google Acquisition," *New York Times*, March 3, 2016.

53 There are cases where firms experience a crisis, identify the need to change their cultures, and then fail to do so. NASA, after the *Challenger* space shuttle disaster, claimed that it was going to become a "safety first" culture where its employees felt comfortable voicing any concerns they had with the safety of a mission. Years later, the agency experienced another shuttle disaster, and an analysis of the *Columbia* disaster concluded that NASA's culture had not changed a great extent after the *Challenger* tragedy. See Marc S. Gerstein and Robert B. Shaw, "Organizational Bystanders," *People and Strategy* 31 (2008), 47–54.

54   Caroline Chen and Cynthia Koons, "Valeant Guts Board as It Shifts Strategy, Attempts Fresh Start," *Washington Post*, May 2, 2016.

55   Xiao-Ping Chen, "Company Culture and Values Are the Lifelines of Alibaba: An Interview with Jack Ma, Founder and Executive," *Executive Perspectives*, August 2013, www.iacmr.org/V2/Publications/CMI/LP021101_EN.pdf.

56   The individual most responsible for the groupthink concept is Irving Janis. See *Victims of Groupthink* (Boston: Houghton Mifflin, 1972); *Groupthink: Psychological Studies of Policy Decisions and Fiascoes* (Boston: Houghton Mifflin, 1982); *Crucial Decisions: Leadership in Policymaking and Crisis Management* (New York: The Free Press, 1989).

57   Matt Palmquist, "The Dangers of Too Much Workplace Cohesion," *strategy+business*, February 10, 2015.

58   Sean Wise, "Can a Team Have Too Much Cohesion? The Dark Side to Network Density," *European Management Journal* 32 (2014), 703–11, www.sciencedirect.com/science/journal/02632373/32/5.

59   Edward O. Welles, "Lost in Patagonia: Yvon Chouinard's Ambitious Social Mission," *Inc.*, August 1, 1992.

60   Adam Waytz, "The Limits of Empathy," *Harvard Business Review* January–February (2016).

61   Rob Cross, Reb Rebele, and Adam Grant, "Collaborative Overload," *Harvard Business Review,* January-February (2016); Radostina K. Purvanova and John P. Muros, "Gender Differences in Burnout: A Meta-Analysis," *Journal of Vocational Behavior* 77 (2010), 168–85. Madeline E. Heilman and Julie J. Chen, "Same Behavior, Different Consequences: Reactions to Men's and Women's Altruistic Citizenship Behavior," *Journal of Applied Psychology* 90 (2005), 431–41.

62   The quote is from Adam Grant and Sheryl Sandberg, "Madam C.E.O., Get Me a Coffee," *New York Times*, February 16, 2016.

63   Barry Johnson, *Polarity Management*, HRD PRess; 2014.

64   Robert Bruce Shaw interview.

65   Ed Catmull, CEO of Pixar, notes the downside of moving too quickly on underperformers on those who remain: "It makes them think, 'oh, if I screw up, they're going to remove me.' So the cost to the organization of moving quickly on somebody is higher than it is if you let the person go on too long. You make the change when the need for it becomes obvious to other people. Then you can do it. I will admit that there are a couple of times, though, that we waited too long. This is a hard part of managing." From "Staying One Step Ahead at Pixar: An Interview with Ed Catmull," *McKinsey Quarterly*, March 2016.

66   Robert Freed Bales, a pioneer in the research on teams, describes what

he calls task-oriented roles (focusing on who contributed the best ideas for solving a particular team problem) and process-oriented roles (focusing on who helps sustain the group morale and keep it moving forward).

Chapter 2: Foster a Shared Obsession

1   Noted in Yvon Chouinard, *Let My People Go Surfing: The Education of a Reluctant Businessman* (New York: Penguin Books, 2006)

2   Chouinard hates the concept fashion for two reasons: it encourages people to value style over substance and it suggests that clothing is disposable. See John Swansburg, "Where Fashion Is the F-Word," *Slate*, March 15, 2012.

3   Emily Rabin, "Don't Get Mad, Get Yvon," *Greenbiz*, October 28, 2004, www.greenbiz.com/news/2004/10/28/dont-get-mad-get-yvon.

4   Estimated 2015 Patagonia revenue based on a 2013 company report listing revenue at that time and then extrapolating a projected growth rate of 15 percent a year.

5   Edward O. Welles, "Lost in Patagonia: Yvon Chouinard's Ambitious Social Mission," *Inc.*, August 1, 1992. The company, after reaching $100 million in sales, reduced its workforce by 20 percent—letting go of friends and friends of friends, in Chouinard's words. The company planned on 50% growth but, because of a recession, achieved 30% growth.

6   Robert Bruce Shaw interview.

7   See the Patagonia Annual Benefit Corporation Report, Fiscal Year 2013. The firm states that its goal is to cause no unnecessary harm to the planet by continually seeking to reduce "the impact of its operations in water use, energy use, greenhouse gas emissions, chemical use, toxicity and waste." www.patagonia.com/pdf/en_US/bcorp_annual_report_2014.pdf.

8   The ad reads, "The most challenging, and important, element of the Common Threads Initiative is this: to lighten our environmental footprint, everyone needs to consume less. Businesses need to make fewer things but of higher quality. Customers need to think twice before they buy." www.adweek.com/news/advertising-branding/ad-day-patagonia -136745.

9   Chouinard, *Let My People Go Surfing: The Education of a Reluctant Businessman*, Loc 320 on ebook.

10   A colleague noted that Chouinard had such a strong focus on quality that it resulted in ignoring other business considerations. "I remember when we'd get shirts back with the buttons fallen off. Yvon would be ripped. You wouldn't want to be around him when those shirts came in. . . . He's a tyrant on that stuff—to the point of saying, 'I don't care what it costs, as long as the buttons don't fall off,' even if that meant sales went from 10,000 to 5,000 units. What was important to him was that the 5,000 units out there be fantastic." Edward O. Welles, "Lost in Patagonia: Yvon Chouinard's Ambitious Social Mission" *Fast Company*, August 1, 1992

11   Chouinard applies quality to every element of how the company functions. He notes, "I don't think it's possible to make a great quality product without having a great quality work environment. So it's linked— quality product, quality customer service, quality workplace, quality of life for your employees, even quality of life for all living things on this planet. If you miss any one piece, there's a good chance you'll miss it all." (Presented at the Conference on Corporate Citizenship, Georgetown University, Washington, D.C., May 16, 1996, clinton6.nara. gov/1996/05/1996-05-16-white-house-conference-on-corporate-citizenship.html.)

12   Josh Barro, "Sorry, but Your Favorite Company Can't Be Your Friend," *New York Times*, December 11, 2015.

13   "Why Evil Is Better in Business (or Is It?)," *Inc.*, March 2016, www.inc.com/magazine/201603/inc-staff/kevin-oleary-adam-lowry-debate-mission-vs-profit.html. Milton Friedman says the same when he maintains that "the business of business is business."

14   Alexandra Jacobs, "Happy Feet: Inside the Online Shoe Utopia," *New Yorker*, September 14, 2009. Zappos is now owned by Amazon, which has a very different culture. It will be interesting to see if Zappos becomes more like Amazon over time.

15   Andrew Stanton, director of *Finding Nemo*, commented on the pressure to do a sequel: "I was always 'No sequels, no sequels.' But I had to get on board from a VP standpoint. [Sequels] are part of the necessity of our staying afloat, but we don't want to have to go there for those reasons. We want to go there creatively, so we said [to Disney], 'Can you give us the timeline about when we release them? Because we'd like to release something we actually want to make, and we might not come up with it the year you want it.'" That said, Pixar has made a number of sequels— most of them of very high quality. See Rebecca Keegan, "With 'Despicable Me 2' and More, Movies Revisit the Sequel Debate," *Los Angeles Times*, July 5, 2013.

16   Walt Disney said, "I don't make movies to make money—I make money to make movies." Quoted in Hayagreeva Rao, Robert Sutton, and Allen P. Webb, "Innovation Lessons from Pixar: An interview with Oscar-Winning Director Brad Bird," *McKinsey Quarterly*, April 2008.

17   Steve Denning, "Making Sense of Zappos and Holacracy," *Forbes*, January 15, 2014. A more detailed description of the approach can be found at Ethan Bernstein et al., "Beyond the Holacracy Hype," *Harvard Business Review* July-August (2016). We will not know for few years if the approach will work at Zappos. My sense is that some elements of it will be retained by the company but it will not survive in its current form due to the complexities of making it work. Another possibility is that it remains as long as Hsieh remains CEO—but is abandoned, in large part, after he departs.

18   There is some debate about the number and cause of employee departures at Zappos. The leadership believes that at least half of the turnover in 2015 was due to people pursuing their personal goals and taking an offer to leave the company (which could be as much as a year's salary depending on an employee's tenure). The leaders also state that the normal turnover in the firm is about 20 percent (indicating the additional turnover in 2015 was only 10 percent). A second reference suggests that 18 percent of the employee population took the company's buyout offer in 2015, with 6 percent citing holacracy as the reason they were leaving. See Gregory Ferenstein, "The Zappos Exodus Wasn't About Holacracy, Says Tony Hsieh," *Fast Company*, January 19, 2016. Also see David Gelles, "The Zappos Exodus Continues After a Radical Management Experiment," *New York Times*, January 13, 2016.

19   See Joseph B. Lassiter and Evan Richardson, "Airbnb," *Harvard Business Review,* September 28, 2011. Also see Max Chafkin, "Airbnb Opens up the World," *Fast Company*, February 2016.

20   Merriam-Webster's definition of obsession: "A state in which someone thinks about someone or something constantly or frequently especially in a way that is not normal; someone or something that a person thinks about constantly or frequently; an activity that someone is very interested in or spends a lot of time doing."

21   "What It Takes to Be As Great As Elon Musk, Steve Jobs, or Richard Branson," *Inc.* Aug 31, 2015

22   See Geoff Colvin, (New York: Portfolio, 2008).

23   Andre Agassi, (New York: Vintage, 2010).

24   See the group's website, www.workaholics-anonymous.org/.

25   Xiao-Ping Chen, "Company Culture and Values Are the Lifelines of Alibaba: An Interview with Jack Ma, Founder and Executive," *Executive Perspectives*, August 2013, www.iacmr.org/V2/Publications/CMI/LP021101_EN.pdf.

26   Graham describes the best founders as being cockroach like—in that they will survive anything, including a nuclear winter, while others perish. See Airbnb, "Conversation with Paul Graham," YouTube. www.youtube.com/watch?v=nrWavoJsEks.

27   "Innovation lessons from Pixar: An interview with Oscar-winning director Brad Bird," *McKinsey Quarterly* Hayagreeva Rao, Robert Sutton, and Allen P. Webb. April 2008.

28   Anthony Lane, "The Fun Factory: Life at Pixar," *New Yorker*, May 16, 2011. Jon Michaud, "Animated by Perfectionism," *New Yorker*, May 16, 2011. "*Snow White* was finished in a panic, and years later Disney was still fretting over the shortcomings of his heroine . . . the wobbles in her construction. 'The bridge on her nose floats all over her face,' he said. He became an industry, but the one thing that links the industrialist, whatever the product, with the auteur, whatever the form, is obsessive pedantry—the will to get things right, whatever the cost may be."

29   "Lessons on Culture and Customer Service from Zappos CEO, Tony Hsieh," *New York Times*. January 9, 2010.

30   Brian Cheskey, "Don't Fuck up the Culture," *Medium*, April 20, 2014, medium.com/@bchesky/dont-fuck-up-the-culture-597cde9ee9d4#.sncu86iwl.

31   Jack Ma, in a letter to his employees, whom he calls the Aliren, noted, "We believe only a group of people who are passionate about the company and are mission-driven will be able to protect the company from external pressure from competition and temptation to seek short-term gains." Juro Osawa, "Softbank, Yahoo Support Alibaba's Partnership Structure," *Wall Street Journal,* September 26, 2013.

32   Paul Graham, a venture capitalist, notes, "The startup founders who end up richest are not the ones driven by money. The ones driven by money take the big acquisition offer that nearly every successful startup gets en route. The ones who keep going are driven by something else. They may not say so explicitly, but they're usually trying to improve the world. Which means people with a desire to improve the world have a natural advantage." Paul Graham blog, November 2014. paulgraham.com/mean. html.

33   *The Anarchist's Cookbook.* Charles Fishman. Fast Company, July 1, 2014. Justin Fox. The HBR Interview: What Is It That Only I Can Do? *Harvard Business Review.* January-February 2011.

34   Paul Graham observes, "It's unlikely that every successful startup improves the world. But their founders, like parents, truly believe they do. Successful founders are in love with their companies. And while this sort of love is as blind as the love people have for one another, it is genuine." Paul Graham blog. Paulgraham.com/mean.html.

35   This higher purpose doesn't mean that Apple hasn't made mistakes over its history, outsourcing some of its manufacturing to plants that operated in manner that calls into question their treatment of employees.

36   Amy Wrzesniewski, C. R. McCauley, P. Rozin, and B. Schwartz, "Jobs, Careers, and Callings: People's Relations to Their Work," *Journal of Research in Personality* 31 (1997), 21–33.

37   Rachel Feintzeig, "I Don't Have a Job: I Have a Higher Calling," *The Wall Street Journal*, February 24, 2015. "[A] survey by the company found that employees whose managers talked about KPMG's impact on society were 42.4% more likely to describe the firm as a great place to work. Of those with managers who talked up meaning, 68% indicated they rarely think about looking for a new job outside KPMG; that share fell to 38% for employees whose managers didn't discuss meaning."

38   Jason Snell, "Steve Jobs: Making a Dent in the Universe," *Macworld*, www. macworld.com/article/1162827/steve_jobs_making_a_dent_in_the_ universe.html.

39   Paul Tough, *How Children Succeed: Grit, Curiosity, and the Hidden Power of Character* (New York: Houghton Mifflin Harcourt, 2012), 74.

40   Angela L. Duckworth, "Grit: The Power of Passion and Perseverance," *TED Talk*, May 2013, www.ted.com/talks/angela_lee_duckworth_the_key_to_ success_grit/transcript?language=en. In this talk, she summarizes her findings: "I started studying kids and adults in all kinds of super challenging settings, and in every study my question was, who is successful here and why? My research team and I went to West Point Military Academy. We tried to predict which cadets would stay in military training and which would drop out. We went to the National Spelling Bee and tried to predict which children would advance farthest in competition We partnered with private companies, asking, which of these salespeople is going to keep their jobs? And who's going to earn the most money? In all those very different contexts, one characteristic emerged as a significant predictor of success. And it wasn't social intelligence. It wasn't good looks, physical health, and it wasn't IQ. It was grit."

41 Angela L. Duckworth, Christopher Peterson, Michael D. Matthews, and Dennis R. Kelly, "Grit: Perseverance and Passion for Long-Term Goals," *Journal of Personality and Social Psychology* 92 (2007), 1087–101. For a critical view of the grit concept, see David Denby, "The Limits of 'Grit,'" *New Yorker*, June 21, 2016.

42 Airbnb "Our Commitment to Trust and Safety," blog.airbnb.com/our-commitment-to-trust-and-safety/.

43 Ari Levy, "Airbnb Offers $50,000 Guarantee After User's Home Is Trashed," *Forbes*, August 1, 2011.

Chapter 3: Value Fit over Capabilities

1 Jack Ma of Alibaba notes, "You should find someone who has complementary skills to start a company with. You shouldn't necessarily look for someone successful. Find the right people, not the best people."

2 On average, other cutting-edge firms have an even higher ratio. Patagonia, for example, is reported to receive an average of 900 resumes for every job it fills. Steve Hamm, "A Passion for the Planet," *Bloomberg Magazine*, August 20, 2006.

3 Zappos just did away with the online posting of open jobs. Now the online community Zappos Insiders manages the talent pool for open positions.

4 Jessica Herrin, founder and CEO of the e-commerce apparel firm Stella and Dot, reinforces this point: "I want to hire missionaries, not mercenaries. The challenge, especially when you're growing fast, is to be incredibly fierce about your hiring filters. You have to commit to caring for the culture more than the quarter." Adam Bryant, "Corner Office," *New York Times*, December 13, 2015.

5 See the firm's website for a list of its 10 values: deliveringhappiness.com/book/zappos-core-values/.

6 Interview with Robert Bruce Shaw.

7 Zappos HR Leader interview with Robert Bruce Shaw. Also see Dick Richards, "At Zappos, Culture Pays," *Strategy and Business* 60 (2010).

8 As suggested in this chapter, fit is essential in sustaining a firm's cultural attributes. That said, fit is also important in the satisfaction of those who work in a company or group. Research indicates an employee's fit with a firm's culture is a strong predictor of organizational commitment, job satisfaction, and retention. See Amy L. Kristof-Brown and Erin C. Johnson, "Consequences of Individuals' Fit at Work: A Meta-Analysis of Person-Job, Person-Organization, Person-Group and Person-Supervisor Fit," *Personnel Psychology* 58 (2005), 281–342.

9 Patagonia's founder notes, "Not everyone wants to change the world, but

we want a company to feel like home for those who do. Employees who are drawn to Chouinard Equipment, and later to Patagonia, either shared those values or did not mind working among those who held them." Yvon Chouinard, *Let My People Go Surfing: The Education of a Reluctant Businessman* (New York: Penguin Books, 2006), Loc 2065 in ebook.

10 See Patagonia's Human Resources Director, "Case 4: Patagonia," Greenleaf Publishing Ltd, 1999, 17.

11 See Michael Housman and Dylan Minor, "Toxic Workers," Harvard Business Unit Strategy Working Paper #16-057, www.hbs.edu/faculty/Publication%20Files/16-057_d45c0b4f-fa19-49de-8f1b-4b12fe054fea.pdf.

12 The research on toxic employees does not directly examine cultural fit. Instead, it looks at a range of beliefs and traits that increase the likelihood that an employee will behave in a manner that hurts his or her firm. The indirect findings, however, indicate that attitudes are contagious—that the more toxic employees there are in a group, the more others will follow their destructive behavior. The assumption is that the same is true in regard to those who fail to support a firm's culture and core values. Dylan Minor and Michael Housman examined the impact of toxic workers using a large dataset of nearly 60,000 workers across 11 firms in different industries. Michael Housman and Dylan Minor, "Toxic Workers," Working Paper 16-057, 2015.

13 Phil Knight, the founder of Nike, remained chairman after Perez was hired as CEO and was a visible presence in the company. See Michael Barbaro and Eric Dash, "Another Outsider Falls Casualty to Nike's Insider Culture," *New York Times*, January 24, 2006.

14 Alfred Lin, "Lecture 10: Company Culture and Building a Team, Part I," *Genius*, genius.com/Alfred-lin-lecture-10-company-culture-and-building -a team-part-i-annotated.

15 Glassdoor. Posted 7/15/2013. www.glassdoor.com/Reviews/Employee-Review-Airbnb-RVW2979155.htm

16 Patty McCord, former human resources head of Netflix, quoted in "The Woman Behind the Netflix Culture Doc," firstround.com/review/The-woman-behind-the-Netflix-Culture-doc/.

17 Karen A. Jehn, Gregory B. Northcraft, and Margaret A. Neale, "Why Differences Make a Difference: A Field Study of Diversity, Conflict, and Performance in Workgroups," *Administrative Science Quarterly* 44 (1999), 741–73.

18 "Inside Pixar's Leadership," in *Creative Thinking, Innovation, Management*. scottberkun.com/2010/inside-pixars-leadership/

19 This problem is found in some of the firms profiled in this book. Zappos, for instance, has ten values:
   1. Deliver WOW through Service
   2. Embrace and Drive Change
   3. Create Fun and a Little Weirdness
   4. Be Adventurous, Creative, and Open-Minded
   5. Pursue Growth and Learning
   6. Build Open and Honest Relationships with Communication
   7. Build a Positive Team and Family Spirit

8. Do More with Less

9. Be Passionate and Determined

10. Be Humble

See also: "See Diverse Teams Feel Less Comfortable—and That's Why They Perform Better., David Rock, Heidi Grant Halvorson and Jacqui Grey. *Harvard Business Review,* September 23, 2016.

20   Andrew M. Carton, Chad Murphy, Jonathan R. Clark, "A (Blurry) Vision of the Future: How Leader Rhetoric About Ultimate Goals Influences Performance," *Academy of Management Journal* 57 (2014): 1544–70.

21   Edgar H. Schein, *Organizational Culture and Leadership* (San Francisco: Jossey-Bass, 2010).

22   Jessica Rohmanm, "Leading Culture During Rapid Growth: A Conversation with Whole Foods Market Co-CEO Walter Robb," *Great Place to Work*, www.greatplacetowork.com/storage/documents/interviews/gptw-whole_foods_interview.pdf.

23   Adam Bryant, "Brian Chesky of Airbnb, on Scratching the Itch to Create," *New York Times*, October 11, 2014.

24   Adam Byant. "Can You Pass a C.E.O. Test?" *New York Times*. March 13, 2009.

25   Tina Fey, comedian and executive producer of the TV show *30 Rock*, describes her philosophy for hiring writers: "Don't hire anyone you wouldn't want to run into in the hallway at three in the morning . . . . We work long hours on these shows, and, no matter how funny someone's writing sample is, if that person is too talkative or needy or angry to deal with by the printer in the middle of the night, steer clear. That must be how I got through that first job interview. I was not dynamic, but at least I wasn't nuts." Tina Fey, "Lessons from Late Night," *New Yorker*, March 14, 2011.

26   "How to Test a New Hire for Core Values," *Inc.* April 28, 2010

27   Adam Bryant, "Your Opinions Are Respected (and Required)," *New York Times*, August 6, 2011.

28   An interesting study examined the fit between a CEO's leadership style and the culture of the firm that he or she is leading. The authors found that the best outcomes occurred when a leader brought what his or her culture was lacking (e.g., a high results leader was beneficial to a relationship focused culture and a high relationship leader was beneficial to a task-focused culture). This is described in a new study as the positive effects of dissimilarity. I don't view this research as contradicting the need for cultural fit; instead, the findings underscore the need for both results and relationships within a firm or team. See "Do Similarities or Differences Between CEO Leadership and Organizational Culture Have a More Positive Effect on Firm Performance? A Test of Competing Predictions," Chad A. Hartnell, Angelo J. Kinicki, Lisa Schurer Lambert, Mel Fugate, and Patricia Doyle Corner. *Journal of Applied Psychology*. 2016, V. 101, #6, 846-861.

Chapter 4: Focus More, Then Less

1   Brian Chesney, CEO of Airbnb, comments on the early mistakes of trying to do too much. "We probably lost six months," he says. "There are so many things we can do; the most challenging part of this is to figure out what not to do." Jessi Hempel, "Airbnb: More than a Place to Crash," *Fortune*, May 3, 2012.

2   Rolfe Winkler and Douglas MacMillan, "The Secret Math of Airbnb's $24 Billion Valuation," *Wall Street Journal*, June 17, 2015.

3   Airbnb Faces Growing Pains as It Passes 100 Million Guests. Max Chafkin and Eric Newcomer. *Bloomberg Businessweek*. July 11, 2016. One Wall Street firm projects that Airbnb will book one billion rooms per year by 2025. The scale of the company is further illustrated by its having 40,000 rooms for rent just in Paris.

4   Reed Hastings, when asked about taking time to establish his firm's cultural principles, noted that during the first four years, Netflix had only one priority, which was to avoid bankruptcy. The company went from having $100 million in startup funding to $5 million before it turned profitable. Airbnb and Netflix were focused on survival.

5   Austin Carr, "Inside Airbnb's Grand Hotel Plans," *Fast Company*, March 17, 2014. The CEO noted about his firm's annual objectives, "If you can't fit it on a page, you're not simplifying it enough . . . . I told my team they have to put the entire plan on a page this big by next week—same size font."

6   "PandoMonthly: Fireside Chat with Airbnb CEO Brian Chesky," *Pando Daily*, January 14, 2013, www.youtube.com/watch?v=6yPfxcqEXhE.

7   Carr, "Inside Airbnb's Grand Hotel Plans."

8   Owen Thomas, "How Airbnb Manages Not to Manage Engineers," *Readwrite*, June 5, 2014, readwrite.com/hack.

9   See Airbnb's website: "Making this environment possible requires a few things. Engineers are involved in goal-setting, planning and brainstorming for all projects, and they have the freedom to select which projects they work on. They also have the flexibility to balance long and short term work, creating business impact while managing technical debt. Does this mean engineers just do whatever they want? No. They work to define and prioritize impactful work with the rest of their team including product managers, designers, data scientists and others." nerds.airbnb. com/engineering-culture-airbnb/.

10   Own Thomas. "How Airbnb Manages Not to Manage Engineers."

11   The importance of experience in Airbnb is suggested when realizing that the head of what most firms call *human resources* is called the *head of employee experience* at Airbnb. His job is to enrich what employees experience at Airbnb—creating a sense of belonging through a wide range of factors, including the design of the workspace, communication and education efforts, the food in the company cafeteria, and a variety of recognition and reward programs.

12   Thomas, "How Airbnb Manages Not to Manage Engineers."

13   These questions are similar to those proposed by Peter Drucker in his

famous five questions in *The Five Most Important Questions You Will Ever Ask About Your Organization* (San Francisco: Jossey-Bass, 2008).

14   "Top Three CEO Bindspots," *Build*, December 5, 2011.

15   Vijay Govindarajan and Anil K. Gupta, "Building an Effective Global Business Team," *MIT Sloan Management Review* Summer (2001).

16   "Netflix Culture: Freedom and Responsibility," Internal presentation, available at www.slideshare.net/reed2001/culture-1798664.

17   Ibid.,

18   "The Woman Behind the Netflix Culture Doc," firstround.com/review/The-woman-behind-the-Netflix-Culture-doc/.

19   See Paul Adler, Charles Heckscher, and Laurence Prusak, "Building a Collaborative Enterprise," *Harvard Business Review,* July-August (2011). They write, "Indeed, we have found that the patience and skill required to create and maintain a sense of common purpose are rare in corporate hierarchies, particularly given that it is not a set-it-and-forget-it process. The purpose must be continually redefined as markets and clients evolve, and members of the community need to be constantly engaged in shaping and understanding complex collective missions. That kind of participation is costly and time-consuming."

20   David A. Nadler and Janet L. Spencer, *Executive Teams* (San Francisco: Jossey Bass, 1998).

21   Yvon Chouinard, *Let My People Go Surfing: The Education of a Reluctant Businessman* (New York: Penguin Books, 2006), Loc 916 in ebook.

22   This, of course, is within the ethical and procedural practices of a company. It is not a "results at any cost" mentality.

23   One researcher, David Rock of the NeuroLeadership Institute, describes a role of shared objectives as follows: "If you can create shared goals among people, you create a strong "in" group quite quickly. When you identify a shared goal, you turn an 'out' group into an 'in' group." Adam Bryant, "A Boss's Challenge: Have Everyone Join the 'In' Group," *New York Times*, March 23, 2013.

24   The CEO of Sparta Systems notes, "I've learned to be incredibly clear about what we're trying to do, how we're going to get there and the outcomes I want from the team. And then when I get that team in place, they can cascade the goals down through the organization so that the front-line people know exactly where we're going. I'll say, 'If you can't see how what you're doing today fits my scorecard, then you need to talk to your boss, because we're misaligned.' If you don't have that, then people go off in a lot of directions. They do a lot of work, but they are not really getting to the result that you're looking for with the company." Adam Bryant, "Eileen Martinson on Clarity of Leadership," *New York Times*, January 9, 2014.

25   Some groups go too far in delineating "who owns what," resulting in a mechanical process of dubious value. The best known tool for those who go down this path is called a RACI—which is a template that allows people to specify the roles of various individuals and groups in regard to specific decisions.

26   This past year, domestic DVDs accounted for just over 8 percent of the firm's revenue.

27   Greylock Partners, "Blitzscaling 18: Brian Chesky on Launching Airbnb and the Challenges of Scale," November 30, 2015, www.youtube.com/watch?v=W608u6sBFpo.

28   See Scott Berkun, "How Do You Build a Culture of Healthy Debate?" June 28, 2013, scottberkun.com/2013/how-to-build-a-culture-of-healthy-debate/.

29   Reed Hastings, CEO of Netflix, asks a slightly different question but with the same intent: "How would the company be different if you were CEO?"

30   Clifton Leaf, "Pixar's Ed Catmull: If Something Works, You Shouldn't Do It Again," Fortune, July 14, 2015.

31   Drake Baer, "This Is Innovation: Tippling at Whole Foods," *Fast Company*, April 5, 2013.

32   "Original Streamed Series Top Binge Viewing Survey for First Time," TiVo Press Release, June 30, 2015, pr.tivo.com/manual-releases/2015/Original-Streamed-Series-Top-Binge-Viewing-Survey.

33   2004 Founders' IPO Letter. https://abc.xyz/investor/founders-letters/2004/ipo-letter.html

34   Nicholas Carlson, "The 'Dirty Little Secret' About Google's 20% Time, According to Marissa Mayer," *Business Insider*, January 14, 2015.

35   See Laszlo Bock, *Work Rules! Insights from Inside Google That Will Transform How You Live and Lead*, Kindle Edition, 2015.

36   Jared M. Spool, "Goods, Bads and Dailies," *UIE*, October 3, 2012, articles.uie.com/great_critiques/.

Chapter 5: Push Harder, Push Softer

1   The concept of hard and soft edges is from Rich Karlgaard's book *The Soft Edge: Where Great Companies Find Lasting Success* (San Francisco: Jossey-Bass, 2014).

2   Note that *hard* and *soft* are not the same as *strong* and *weak*. Strong corporate cultures are those where there is a high level of consistency in what people think and feel. Weak cultures are those where there is wide variation in what people think and feel. Strong is generally better than weak unless the company's culture is out of sync with what is needed to be competitive (in that case, people share a set of beliefs that are dysfunctional).

3   Edgar H. Schein, *Organizational Culture and Leadership* (San Francisco: Jossey-Bass, 2010).

4   While the difference may be subtle, I think of beliefs as being based on deeper-level cognitive assumptions. Feelings, in turn, are based on deeper-level, more visceral emotions.

5   Howard Schultz and Joanne Gordon, *Onward: How Starbucks Fought for Its Life without Losing Its Soul* (New York: Rodale, 2012), 117.

6   Ibid. Also, Mark Bonchek, "How to Build a Strategic Narrative," *Harvard Business Review,* March 25, 2016, 141–42.

7   There is a long-standing debate on the difference between organizational culture and climate. Some authors distinguish between the two by arguing that culture is "the way we do things around here" while climate is "how it feels to work here." Most definitions, however, are more complex and include different views in regard to the causal relationship between culture and climate (for example, does culture determine the climate?). My position is that culture includes climate and the emotional feelings of people at work. These feelings are not the surface of work life but the most fundamental aspect of how a company operates. For a detailed exploration of culture and climate, see Benjamin Schneider, Mark G. Ehrhart, and William H. Macey, "Organizational Climate and Culture," *The Annual Review of Psychology* 64 (2012), 61–88; Daniel R. Denison, "What Is the Difference Between Organizational Culture and Organizational Climate? A Native's Point of View on a Decade of Paradigm Wars," *The Academy of Management Review* 21 (1996), 619–54.

8   Mollie West, "Ideo: The 7 Most Important Hires for Creating a Culture of Innovation," *Fast Company*, April 19, 2016.

9   "Best Places to Work," *Glassdoor*, www.glassdoor.com/Best-Places-to-Work-LST_KQ0,19.htm. The rankings are based on a total of 1.6 million employee reviews across all companies in the database.

10   Consider that 50 percent of the American population is now single. Nearly the same percent of women don't have children. While this doesn't mean that work becomes all important to these people, we can assume that in some cases work will play a more central role in their lives. Nor am I suggesting that those who are married or with children view work as any less important than others—only that those who are single and without children have fewer demands on their time and attention.

11   Kim Cameron, Carlos Mora, Trevor Leutscher, and Margaret Calarco, "Effects of Positive Practices on Organizational Effectiveness," *The Journal of Applied Behavioral Science* 47 (2011), 266–308. See also Emma Seppala, "Positive Teams Are More Productive," *Harvard Business Review*, March 18, 2015.

12   "Staying One Step Ahead at Pixar: An Interview with Ed Catmull," *McKinsey Quarterly*, March 2016.

13   Sonia Kolesnikov-Jessop, "Spotlight: Jack Ma, Co-Founder of Alibaba.com," *New York Times*, January 5, 2007.

14   Caitlin Roper, "Big Hero 6 Proves It: Pixar's Gurus Have Brought the Magic Back to Disney Animation," *Wired*, October 21, 2014.

15   Ibid.

16   Note that this is my interpretation of each firm's culture based on their own statements, articles, and books on how these companies operate and my own interviews. Also note that the cultural themes outlined are different than the missions of these firms—culture speaks to the experience of working in a company versus the mission to which each firm is dedicated. Mission and culture are related but not the same.

17   "Netflix Culture: Freedom and Responsibility." Internal presentation, slide 61, available at www.slideshare.net/reed2001/culture-1798664.

18   People in certain Netflix areas, such as finance, can't take time during a critical period at the beginning or end of a quarter due to the demands of the generating an earnings report. Also, people need to inform human resources if they are going to take more than 30 days off at any point in time.

19   Patty McCord, "How Netflix Reinvented HR," *Harvard Business Review,* January-February (2014).

20   Whole Foods Market website. Creating the high trust organization. http://www.wholefoodsmarket.com/blog/john-mackeys-blog/creating-high-trust-organization

21   "Netflix Culture: Freedom and Responsibility," slide 22: "Unlike many companies, we practice: adequate performance gets a generous severance package." slide 111: "... We don't want employees to feel competitive with each other. We want all of our employees to be 'top 10%' relative to the pool of global candidates. We want employees to help each other, and they do."

22   "Netflix Culture: Freedom and Responsibility," slide 38.

23   Jena McGregor, "Meet Alibaba's Jack Ma," *Washington Post,* May 6, 2014.

24   From the Zappos LinkedIn website posting.

25   A kayak trip Chouinard took in 2015 with a group of his friends resulted in the death of Chouinard's fellow entrepreneur Doug Tompkins. See Stewart M. Green, "Doug Tompkins Dies in Kayaking Accident in Patagonia," *Alpinist,* December 9, 2015.

26   Robert Bruce Shaw interview.

27   Jonny Elwyn, "Lessons in Creativity from Pixar's Top Creatives," *Premium Beat,* March 28, 2014.

28   Ed Catmull, "How Pixar Fosters Collective Creativity," *Harvard Business Review* September (2008).

29   Zappos Family Core Value #7: Build a positive team and family spirit, www.zapposinsights.com/about/zappos/our-unique-culture.

30   Zappos Family Core Value #7.

31   Steven Rosenbaum, "The Happiness Culture: Zappos Isn't a Company—It's a Mission," *Fast Company,* June 4, 2010.

32   David Foster Wallace, "This Is Full Water," commencement speech to Kenyon College class of 2005, www.youtube.com/watch?v=8CrOL-ydFMI.

Chapter 6: Take Comfort in Discomfort

1   Beth Comstock of General Electric says to her team members, "Tell me one thing I don't want to hear. It's O.K. to give me some bad news. In fact, I want it." Adam Bryant, "Beth Comstock of General Electric: Granting Permission to Innovate," *New York Times,* June 17, 2016. The U.S. military has a slang phrase indicating a similar approach: "Embrace the suck."

2   Margaret Mead's famous remark about groups applies to extreme teams:

"Never doubt that a small group of thoughtful, committed citizens can change the world. Indeed, it's the only thing that ever has." Nancy C. Lutkehaus, *Margaret Mead: The Making of an American Icon* (Princeton: Princeton University Press, 2008), 261.

3   Jack Ma, when asked what drove the success of his company, noted that it had three essential attributes—no money, no technology, and no plan. For a detailed account of the battle with eBay, see Duncan Clark, *Alibaba: The House That Jack Ma Built* (New York: Harper Collins, 2016), Loc 262 of ebook.

4   eBay, in 2006, folded its operations into a joint venture with a Chinese firm, Tom Online. eBay retained a 49 percent share in the venture but, in essence, had pulled out of the market.

5   The comedian Jon Stewart noted after Alibaba's massive public stock offering that "The communists just beat us at capitalism."

6   Alibaba also provides a range of services in addition to its products, some of which are quite interesting. For example, a customer can hire a date to attend a social event.

7   Neil Gough and Alexandra Stevenson, "The Unlikely Ascent of Jack Ma, Alibaba's founder," *New York Times*, May 8, 2014.

8   Alibaba is on track to be the world's first trillion-dollar business (the value of annual transactions through its various platforms in dollars). See Rex Crum, "Alibaba's Jack Ma Talks Big, Even Trillion-Dollar Big," *Fortune*, June 12, 2015.

9   See Julie Wulf, "Alibaba Group," *Harvard Business Review*, April 26, 2010.

10   From "Alibaba Culture & Values. Passion: We Expect Our People to Approach Everything with Fire in their Belly and Never Give Up on Doing What They Believe Is Right," www.alibabagroup.com/en/about/culture.

11   Dai Tian, "Exclusive Look Inside Alibaba's 'Kung Fu' Culture," *China Daily. com*, October 10, 2014.

12   Charles Clover, "Method in the Madness of the Alibaba Cult," *Financial Times*, September 7, 2014.

13   Erving Goffman, *The Presentation of Self in Everyday Life* (New York: Random House, 1959).

14   Adam Bryant, "Xerox's New Chief Tries to Redefine Its Culture," *New York Times*, February 20, 2010. Burns notes: "When we're in the family, you don't have to be as nice as when you're outside of the family." She says, "I want us to stay civil and kind, but we have to be frank—and the reason we can be frank is because we are all in the same family." Also see Richard Feloni, "Xerox CEO Ursula Burns Explains the Problem with a Corporate Culture That Is Too Nice," *Business Insider*, March 5, 2016.

15   Adam Bryant, *The Corner Office: Indispensable and Unexpected Lessons from CEOs on How to Lead and Succeed* (New York: Times Books, 2011), 218.

16   George Packer, comment, *New Yorker*, July 5, 2010.

17   Hayagreeva Rao, Robert Sutton, and Allen P. Webb, "Innovation Lessons from Pixar: An Interview with Oscar-Winning Director Brad Bird," *McKinsey Quarterly*, April 2008.

18   Gregory Bateson, *Steps to an Ecology of Mind: a Revolutionary Approach to Man's Understanding of Himself* (New York: Ballantine Books, 1972).

19   See Thomas Kilmann Conflict Survey, www.kilmanndiagnostics.com/overview-thomas-kilmann-conflict-mode-instrument-tki.

20   Rao, Sutton, and Webb, "Innovation Lessons from Pixar: An Interview with Oscar-Winning Director Brad Bird."

21   Conflict can also be with other groups within a company as well as with those outside of a company. Internally, the best teams face conflict across groups and do so with the political and organizational savviness needed to achieve results. There are teams that develop a capability to deal with conflict internally but lack the skills needed to effectively surface and resolve conflict with other teams inside their organization. For an excellent analysis of how teams need to engage other organizational groups, see Deborah Ancona and Henrik Bresman, "X-Teams: How to Build Teams That Lead, Innovate and Succeed," *Harvard Business Review Press*, 2007.

22   Scott Berkun notes, "Many talented organizations produce little of merit because of how sensitive people are of criticism, and the fear of offending people or being offended trumps everything else." "How Do You Build a Culture of Healthy Debate," June 28, 2013, scottberkun.com/2013/how-to-build-a-culture-of-healthy-debate/.

23   Ed Catmull, (New York: Random House, 2014).

24   Ed Catmull, CEO of Pixar, notes, "It is the nature of things—in order to create, you must internalize and almost become the project for a while, and that near-fusing with the project is an essential part of its emergence. But it is also confusing. Where once a movie's writer/director had perspective, he or she loses it. Where once he or she could see a forest, now there are only trees."

25   One of my colleagues describes this as "Rearranging the deck chairs on the *Titanic*."

26   See Ruth Wageman and J. Richard Hackman, "What Makes Teams of Leaders Leadable?" In *Handbook of Leadership Theory and Practice*, chapter 17 (Boston: HBR Press, 2010). The authors look at the role of leaders in surfacing that which people want to ignore, as well as designing the team to encourage the same.

27   For more suggestions on how to make this happen, see Jean L. Kahwajy, Kathleen M. Eisenhardt, and L. J. Bourgeois III, "How Management Teams Can Have a Good Fight," *Harvard Business Review* July-August, 1997.

28   See Kristin Behfar, "How We Fight at Work, and Why it Matters," *Strategy and Business*, March 2, 2015. She has a two-dimensional model of how people manage conflict (being high or low in directness and high or low in what she calls "oppositional intensity").

29   Daniel Kahneman and Gary Klein, "Strategic Decisions: When Can You Trust Your Gut?" Interview in *McKinsey Quarterly*, March 2010.

30   Daniel Kahneman, *Thinking, Fast and Slow* (New York: Farrar, Straus and Giroux, 2013).

31   Charlan J. Nemeth, Bernard Personnaz, Marie Personnaz, and Jack A. Goncalo, "The Liberating Role of Conflict in Group Creativity: A Study in Two Countries," *European Journal of Social Psychology*, 34 (2004), 365–74. See also *Annals of Ideas*, January 30, 2012 issue. Jonah Lehrer, "Groupthink: The Brainstorming Myth," *New Yorker*, January 30, 2012.

32   Cited in David Burkus, "How Criticism Creates Innovative Teams," *Harvard Business Review*, July 22, 2013.

33   David Burkus, "Why Fighting for Our Ideas Makes Them Better," *99U*, 99u. com/articles/7224/why-fighting-for-our-ideas-makes-them-better.

34   Jump Associates, "The Inside Story: 5 Secrets to Pixar's Success," *Fast Company*, September 14, 2011, www.fastcodesign.com/1665008/the-inside-story-5-secrets-to-pixar-s-success.

35   Burkus, "Why Fighting for Our Ideas Makes Them Better."

36   Anita Williams Woolley, Christopher F. Chabris, Alex Pentland, Nada Hashmi, and Thomas W. Malone, "Evidence for a Collective Intelligence Factor in the Performance of Human Groups," *Science*, 330 (2010), 686–88.

37   The test probes the degree to which people can assess the emotions of others by looking at photographs of their faces. Those who scored higher on the test were more accurate in their assessments of another's emotional state.

38   Amy Edmondson, "Psychological Safety and Learning Behavior in Work Teams," *Administrative Science Quarterly*, 44 (1999): 350–83.

39   Edmondson, "Psychological Safety and Learning Behavior in Work Teams," 354.

40   Charles Duhigg, "What Google Learned From Its Quest to Build the Perfect Team," *New York Times*, February 25, 2016.

41   An important way of viewing these teams involves trust. High-trust teams are those where people respect their peers for their capabilities and feel supported by them as individuals. This combination produces higher levels of trust, which, in turn, provides an environment that can tolerate higher levels of conflict. In contrast, low-trust teams have difficulty surfacing conflict and then resolving it productively because people withhold information or points of view from those they don't trust. See my book *Trust in the Balance* (San Francisco: Jossey Bass, 1997).

42   Yvon Chouinard believes that extremes are also beneficial in one's personal life. He has engaged in a variety of risky outdoor activities, such as mountain climbing and kayaking, his entire life

43   See Roger Schwarz, "Get a Dysfunctional Team Back on Track," *Harvard Business Review*. hbr.org/2013/11/get-a-dysfunctional-team-back-on-track

Chapter 7: Teams at the Extremes

1   Alfred North Whitehead wrote, "Without adventure, civilization is in full decay."

2   Ed Catmull at Pixar. Brian Chesky at Airbnb. Yvon Chouinard at Patagonia. Reed Hastings at Netflix. Tony Hsieh at Zappos. Jack Ma at Alibaba. John Mackey at Whole Foods. Note that these founders had at least one partner in the creation of their companies.

3   In the movie *Whiplash*, the protagonist yells at his most promising student, "There are no two words in the English language more harmful than 'good job.'"

4   See Richard Pascale, Mark Millemann, and Linda Gioja, *Surfing the Edge of Chaos: The Laws of Nature and The New Laws of Business* (New York: Crown Business, 2001).

5   "Staying One Step Ahead at Pixar: An Interview with Ed Catmull," *McKinsey Quarterly*, March 2016.

6.   See Wendy K. Smith, Marianne W. Lewis, and Michael L. Tushman, "'Both/And' Leadership," *Harvard Business Review* May (2016). The authors examine what they describe as the paradoxes of effective leadership, which stand in contrast to an "either/or" approach.

7   Very strong on results or relationships meant that a leader was in the top quartile of ratings provided by over 60,000 employees. See John H. Zenger and Joseph R. Folkman, *The Extraordinary Leader* (New York: McGraw Hill, 2009), 144.

8   One way of understanding the complications of managing results and relationships is to look at the expectations that each creates in a team, organization, or even with customers. Research indicates that leaders and groups that emphasize the importance of results and relationships are judged more harshly when they fall short of the expectations they have created in these areas. A study by Pankaj Aggarwal, for example, indicates that people who view a company as being "personal and warm" in its interactions with them are harsher in their judgments when those firms act in a manner that they believe is driven by financial results. In essence, these firms suffer because they create an expectation ("we care about you") that is then violated ("we care about profits"). In a similar manner, we can see how firms or teams that emphasize a results orientation are viewed more harshly when they retain or promote people whose performance is substandard. In essence, people in these situations see the firm or its leaders as being hypocritical. For the study noted above that looked at this dynamic in terms of customer perceptions, see Pankaj Aggarwal, "The Effects of Brand Relationship Norms on Consumer Attitudes and Behavior," *Journal of Consumer Research* 31 (2004).

9.   This table builds directly on the ideas of Amy Edmondson in her well-respected work on psychological safety. In particular, she presents a similar table to the one presented here. In it, Edmondson describes different team cultures, or what she calls *zones*. She has "ambitious goals" on one axis of her table and "psychological safety" on another. She then describes four types of teams: Learning Teams, Anxious Teams, Comfortable Teams, and Apathetic Teams. See "Competitive Imperative of Learning," *Harvard Business Review,* July-August (2008).

10   Richard Hackman argues that the common perception that teams, over time, become complacent is not supported by the research findings (with only one exception, which involves R&D teams). My point is not to suggest a trend toward increased complacency; my point is that teams differ considerably in the degree to which they value results or relationships. See Diane Coutu, "Why Teams Don't Work," *Harvard Business Review* May (2009).

11. A study by the consulting group McKinsey asked senior managers about the most important factors in managing their transitions into new roles. Of the 1,200 people polled, 87 percent indicated that it was very or extremely important to "create a shared vision and alignment around strategic direction across the organization" (the highest rated item in the survey). See "Ascending to the C-Suite," *McKinsey Quarterly*, April 2015.

12. Ed Schein is the go-to authority on corporate culture. See *Organizational Culture and Leadership* (San Francisco: Jossey-Bass, 2010).

13 See Jesse Sostrin, "Follow the Contradictions," *Strategy and Business*, June 6, 2016.

14 Paul Graham, venture capitalist, suggests that most startup firms that fail are not cases of homicide but suicide. His observation applies to many teams as well.

15 See the following, which focuses on cross-functional teams but makes the point regarding underperforming teams: Behnam Tabrizi, "75% of Cross-Functional Teams Are Dysfunctional," *Harvard Business Review*, June 23, 2015.

16 Processes and rules also exist to protect employees. For instance, firms need to protect their employees from harassment by supervisors and coworkers. Policies are put into place to delineate what constitutes harassment and the procedures employees can follow to report, and if possible prevent, such behavior.

17 Richard Hackman notes that the use of a leader's authority to set a team direction "inevitably arouses angst and ambivalence—for the person exercising it and the people on the receiving end." My point is more general in saying that power issues influence a wide range of team behaviors, with the focus here on teams being viewed as a threat by some leaders. See Hackman, "Why Teams Don't Work," *Harvard Business Review* May (2009).

18 Charleen R. Chase and Jon Maner, "Divide and Conquer: When and Why Leaders Undermine the Cohesive Fabric of Their Group," *Journal of Personality and Social Psychology* 107 (2014), 1033–55.

19 Kellogg Insight, "Why Bad Bosses Sabotage Their Teams," *Kellogg School of Management*, January 5, 2015, insight.kellogg.northwestern.edu/article/why-bad-bosses-sabotage-their-teams.

20 Jeff Bezos noted about innovation in product ideas, " To invent you have to experiment, and if you know in advance that it's going to work, it's not an experiment Most large organizations embrace the idea of invention, but are not willing to suffer the string of failed experiments necessary to get there." His insight applies to organizational innovation as well, including new team designs. Amazon SEC Filing;Form 8-K. 4/5/2016.

21 Intellectual breakthroughs, our course, are the result in some cases of individuals working alone. But when putting ideas into action, teams are almost always involved.

INDEX